WITHDRAWN

STOP THE WHALING

WILLIE MACKENZIE

A BEAUTIFUL SPECIAL

First published 2008.

A Beautiful Special from Beautiful Books

www.beautiful-books.co.uk

Beautiful Books Limited
36-38 Glasshouse Street
London W1B 5DL

ISBN 9781905636341

9 8 7 6 5 4 3 2 1

Cover and book design by Studio Dempsey
Set in Franklin Gothic and Schnellfetter
Printed in Great Britain by Quadracolor

For Sonny, Kai, Erin, Crystal and Abbie
may you grow up in a world full of whales

Orca

CONTENTS

Image on preceding page:
Greenpeace activists block the whalers'
aim with a spray of sea water

Image above:
Even the photogenic humpbacks are still
in the whalers' sights, as well as facing
many other threats

Prologue

The vast majority of people don't see whales very often. That's not surprising, as most of us don't spend a lot of time in the ocean, and conversely whales don't get about much on land. When whales do grab our attention it's usually via the news – with reports of animals beaching on shore, or swimming up river attracting crowds of gawping onlookers. But most often the newsworthiness of whales relates to whaling, with images of bloody, harpooned animals pricking the collective conscience of the public, and generating media airtime.

Despite a very public and successful campaign to 'Save the Whale' whaling still happens around the world. To me that's an unacceptable outrage, and made worse because we are also killing whales and their kin in many other less visually dramatic ways too.

Unfortunately news reports are limited, constricted by precious column inches or competing for airtime with the latest celebrity affair – so the point of this book is to try and give an accessible, overall picture of whaling, whales, and the threats they face at our hands. Along the way we'll meet many of the world's different whale species, and briefly consider the shared history of whales and people. We'll then look at the world today, the whaling that is still going on, and the litany of other hazards whales face.

And lastly we will think about the future, what might happen, and how we can help to make sure future generations get to share the planet with these amazing animals too.

This book is too short to cover everything in detail, but hopefully it will give a glimpse of the history and issues surrounding whales and whaling. I make no bones about my own bias, I don't think whaling nowadays is either necessary or justifiable, and the legacy of commercial whaling on the world's population of whales should be enough reason to stop it for good. When taken in the context of what else we are doing to whales and the oceans they live in, continuing to directly hunt them is even less acceptable.

The eye of a baby sperm whale

1 | Big blubber

Size matters

The human heart is about the size of a fist. The heart of a blue whale is the size of a small family car. Whales are mammals, just like we are, and we share many characteristics – we are warm-blooded, slow-growing, breathe air and suckle our babies with milk. But it's the differences that make us appreciate just how well adapted whales are to their life and surroundings in the ocean.

At up to about 30 metres long and weighing up to around 190 tonnes the blue whale is the biggest animal that has ever lived. It's longer and heavier than any dinosaur; a fully-grown elephant could fit on its tongue. If an adult blue whale was ever unfortunate enough to be stuck in London traffic, it would be as long as three and a half double-decker buses, or a Boeing 737 aircraft.

When we think of whales we usually think of these giants and their incomprehensible size. But in fact the family of mammals to which whales belong are not all giants. With approximately 80 species, the group of mammals called cetaceans is whales, dolphins and porpoises – which are supremely adapted for an aquatic life. They range through all of the world's oceans, and even populate some of the bigger river basins. From pole to equator, to the other pole, they are found in all depths and temperatures of water.

Some eat the tiniest creatures in our seas; others eat some of the biggest, including other cetaceans. Some of them travel many thousands of miles between breeding and feeding grounds every year, others stay their whole lives in small areas.

The smallest of the cetaceans are not much over a metre long, and would probably be able to squeeze through the main arteries of a blue whale if they ever found themselves stuck there. Our knowledge of these animals is by no means complete – there is much that we don't know. But what we do know is enough to amaze, enthuse and inspire us. And what we know of our own historical role in exploiting these animals is enough to anger, sadden and repulse us.

What's in a name?

Cetaceans are the only group of mammals to live an entirely aquatic existence, with the notable exception of their distant vegetarian cousins the manatees and dugongs known collectively as 'sirenians'. Both groups' names are results of some rather fanciful beliefs – 'cetaceans' comes from the Greek word for sea monsters, and sirenians are so-called because of an alleged similarity to enchanting mermaids. As adorable as dugongs and manatees are, that's a bit of a stretch.

The very term 'whale' is a bit confusing. In some ways all cetaceans are whales. And scientifically they are split into two distinct groups – the odontocetes ('toothed whales'), and the mysticetes (which technically means 'moustached whales', but refers to whales with hanging baleen plates instead of teeth). The odontocetes are the bigger grouping, containing about 70 species – including sperm whales, dolphins, orcas, belugas, beaked whales and porpoises; but the mysticetes are generally the bigger animals, including the humpback, right, fin and blue whales in their group.

This is further confused by common names – what is known as a dolphin, porpoise, or whale in one part of the world may be called something else elsewhere. Similarly the orca, or killer whale, is actually the largest member of the dolphin family.

For the purposes of this book, and your and my sanity, I will endeavour to keep my references to dolphins, whales, and porpoises as simple and clear as possible. When I talk about whales I will usually be referring to the 'Great whales', the 'big 10' species which are: blue, fin, Bryde's, sei, minke, humpback, gray, bowhead, right and the sperm whale. When I talk about other species I will refer to them by their common English names (and I'll give them a scientific name when we get better acquainted with them in the text – just to be sure!). And when I'm talking about the whole lot, I'll just say 'cetaceans'.

Almost like a hippo

Adaptation for life at sea has meant that cetaceans have undergone some radical changes in the process of evolution. The great Charles Darwin[1] speculated on how species arise whilst considering a bear swimming in the water, mouth agape, to catch insects – he wondered if that was how whales came to be.

Astonishing as it may seem, we know from fossil evidence (especially from Asia) that the evolution of whales can be traced back to carnivorous, hoofed land animals that lived in freshwater swamps in what was the Tethys Sea (an inland sea in roughly the same area as the Mediterranean Sea is today) sometime after the fall of the dinosaurs, some 50 million years ago.

DNA evidence has shown that the closest living relatives to cetaceans are in fact not bears, but hippos. Although well suited for an aquatic life, vegetarian hippos still return to the land to feed. Their portly physique and ease in the water would tend to suggest an obvious affinity with whales – but they are very different.

Keeping in shape

There are of course many air-breathing animals that are adapted for an aquatic life, such as seals, penguins and turtles. There are clear similarities in the body shape of these animals: well streamlined, torpedo-shaped bodies and large 'wing-like' forelimbs that allow them to swim and manoeuvre efficiently.

For warm-blooded animals (mammals and birds) insulation is also an issue because water conducts heat away from the body 25 times quicker than air, and this is especially problematic in colder seas. Sea otters rely on dense fur to keep them warm, but others tend to rely on a thick layer of fat. Being big helps, that's why even the smallest porpoises are quite big by mammal terms. Bigger animals are more efficient at retaining heat. But they also need some insulation, and the smooth-skinned cetaceans have lost their mammalian fur: they rely instead on a thick layer of fat called blubber. It varies between species, but the layer of blubber can be over 50cm thick. In the big whales it generally follows that the 'rounder' whales, like rights, bowheads and humpbacks, have thicker blubber than the slimmer whales like fins, seis, and minkes.

Blubber is such an effective insulator that it actually prevents some species from travelling through warmer seas (they would overheat) leading to distinct populations in northern and southern hemispheres. Along with the lack of support and buoyancy of sea water, the efficiently insulating blubber also causes whales that wash up on beaches to quickly overheat and dehydrate. But the bigger danger from blubber, as we shall see later, is the commercial value that it presented to whalers – as a commodity for worldwide trade.

Blubber is great for keeping warm, but cetaceans face another problem – which is how to keep suitably cool when necessary and how to maintain their body temperature. Some parts of a whale or dolphin are more likely to lose heat than others – and (comparatively) thin fins and tails present a challenge. They have evolved ingenious methods of warming the returning blood from their extremities so that it doesn't bring the internal body temperature down. Even more ingeniously they have a complicated circulatory system that uses cool blood from the fins to keep their testicles from overheating inside their blubber.

Breathing

Breathing is another factor that made whales vulnerable – by venturing above the surface for a precious breath they put themselves at risk of harpoons. But whales, like all mammals, need to breathe. Over time the whales' nostrils have evolved into 'blowholes'. Toothed whales have one, baleen whales have two, and in all species (except for the odd exception of the sperm whale) these have migrated backwards to be on the top of the head. Whales can, of course, hold their breath for a long time, with deep diving species like sperm whales being able to easily last for over an hour between breaths. Amongst other species that time varies, but in the end they all have to surface for air. That normally involves several breaths at the surface and then a big deep breath before they dive again.

Whales are also remarkably efficient when breathing. As humans we exchange about 15% of the air in our lungs when we breathe; in cetaceans the proportion of air exchanged is about 90%. Their amazingly efficient lungs make sure that as much vital oxygen as possible is available to the whales, enabling them to last so long underwater. To make underwater life even more efficacious, the blood of cetaceans is especially efficient in storing oxygen and releasing it slowly during long dives.

It's a common misconception that whales blow water out of their blowholes. They don't. 'Thar she blows!' is not a spout of water, but instead a column of exhaled air mixed with water vapour. The water vapour occurs in two ways – firstly like our own breath on a cold day, the warm breath condenses in contact with colder air and secondly there is often a reservoir of water around the blowhole (baleen whales have a kind of 'splash guard' in front of their blowholes) which is mixed with the exhaled breath – kind of like blowing your nose through a small puddle.

The blows themselves are the traditional way of spotting a whale, and often species can be identified by the shape and size of their blows alone. The blow of a blue whale can reach 9 metres high, the blow of a right whale makes a characteristic V shape (sadly pointing directly towards the unfortunate whale), and the blow of a sperm whale comes out at an angle of 30 degrees!

Getting legless

In London's Natural History Museum the mammals' hall is dominated by a model of a blue whale. Suspended from the ceiling are skeletons of blue, sperm, right, gray and bowhead whales – showing some surprising inside insights into the whales' body plans. The first thing that is striking is the tail. The tail or 'fluke' of a whale is not formed from hind limbs. In fact the broad paddle of a tail that is so essential to a whale's consummate ability to swim and dive is a muscular adaptation at the end of the natural tail. The second thing that strikes you on the skeleton is the hind legs. Of course, there aren't any – but vestigial bones buried deep within the bulk of the whale's body show reminders of legs and a no-longer needed pelvis bone. A reminder, in case we needed one, that whales evolved from four-legged land mammals.

Another striking skeletal reminder exists in the forelimbs, which in cetaceans are manifested as streamlined pectoral fins. Inside these fins are the bones of a mammalian arm and 'hand' – shortened, and with no external features showing, yes – but unmistakable.

Feeding

Whales, dolphins and porpoises all eat other animals. But there is a wide range of marine species that are targeted by the cetaceans and almost no part of the marine food web is untouched. With the notable exception of the orca (which we'll give special attention to in a moment) all whales eat their prey whole. In some cases these are sizeable individual animals, like fish or squid, in other cases that means a big mouthful of smaller prey. The toothed whales tend to eat bigger prey animals (which their teeth help to catch) and tend to eat one at a time. The numbers of teeth, and their size, vary greatly in toothed whales – the toothiest cetaceans are undoubtedly the dolphins, with the record holder being the spinner dolphin with as many as 250 teeth per mouthful. In fact the true way to distinguish a porpoise from a dolphin is by the shape of the teeth (spade-shaped and cone-shaped, respectively). Sperm whale teeth can reach 25cm in length, and weigh over a kilogram each. Some whales that specialise in hunting squid have very few teeth, and it's believed these are actually more important for fighting and competing for mates than for eating.

The notable toothy anomaly is the narwhal (**Monodon monoceros**). These bizarre whales of the extreme north sport one massive tooth that protrudes as a great horny tusk (very occasionally there are two) in males. At up to 3 metres in length, these undoubtedly helped fuel unicorn legends of old. Not quite as spectacular, but equally bizarre are some of the curved tusk-like teeth on the little-known beaked whales. In some species these effectively prevent the mouth from opening properly!

Blue whale gulping a huge mouthful
of prey-laden seawater

In much the same way as we humans eat smaller items by the mouthful, rather than one-at-a-time, so do whales. Baleen whales tend to eat smaller prey – such as small fish, and plankton. To do this they have evolved ingenious methods of corralling food together, and even more remarkable eating equipment. In their mouths hang sheets of 'baleen', made of keratin, like human fingernails or rhinoceros horns. This is coupled with either enormous mouths (in the right and bowhead whales), or just very large mouths (in the rorquals) with pleated 'expandable' throats. In this way these giant creatures take a huge mouthful of seawater and filter the food from the water by sieving it through their baleen. It's like taking a big mouthful of breakfast cereal and spitting the milk back out through gaps in your teeth (please don't try this at home).

Different species have different amounts and types of baleen, from just over a hundred to about 700 plates, ranging from just a few centimetres in length in gray whales to about 3 metres long in bowheads.

This lets them filter different sized organisms, and is somewhat akin to using different sized meshes in fishing nets. The smaller the mesh – the smaller the things you can catch.

The toothed whales find their prey by echolocation, which is essentially a biological version of sonar, also used by bats. By sending out noises that bounce off their surroundings they effectively 'see' with sound. This is a remarkably effective adaptation, allowing them to hunt in darkness and with a great degree of accuracy – many small cetaceans even seem to be able to differentiate between prey species by echolocation.

Some toothed, and one species of baleen whale (grays) feed by 'suction'. For the grays, this enables them to feed on seafloor-dwelling crustaceans and to filter the water and sediment back through their small baleen plates. In the beaked whales, this allows them to slurp up slippery squid in the deep sea without opening their mouths very much (a handy trick if your curvy teeth mean you can't!).

The orca is a special case. Undoubtedly the most exciting

whale for kids everywhere (and I count myself as one of them) – it is blessed with dramatic colouration, fierce teeth, huge fins and a massive reputation. Orcas are also known as 'killer whales', a moniker that they do their best to live up to. They are large oceanic dolphins, and hunt in packs, which means they are often likened to wolves. Their diet is very varied: as a rule, they'll eat whatever they can get their teeth into. Around the world different populations have developed techniques for successfully hunting different prey – such as following shoals of herring, snatching seabirds and seals, or even harassing and killing large whales. However, when attacking large whales, pods of orcas usually just eat some tasty parts of their prey – like the tongue and throat – and leave the rest of the kill behind. Orcas themselves have no known predators to fear, other than us.

Whales don't drink, which is at once seemingly strange and eminently sensible. As (predominantly) ocean-going creatures, their bodies already have to tolerate high levels of salinity, and drinking seawater would not be a good idea! So all of the water that whales need is obtained from the food they eat. This means that a whale deprived of food is likely to dehydrate before it starves, as was the case with the Northern bottlenose whale (**Hyperoodon ampullatus**) that became stranded and died in the River Thames in London in January 2006.

Breeding
The challenges of breeding in water for a mammal are considerable, and cetaceans and sirenians are the only two groups of mammals who have perfected this. The seals, sea lions and walruses by contrast still breed on land often in vast 'rookeries' for safety in numbers. Perhaps unsurprisingly, cetaceans are slow breeders. They grow slowly, mature slowly, gestate for a long time, and the young stay with their mothers for a considerable time too. Indeed in some species it is a bond that is never broken. In cetaceans, sexual maturity tends to occur when animals are between about 5 and 15 years of age. As a rule, single babies are born, although twins and triplets

have been recorded. And baby whales always arrive tail first. When they are born their mother guides them to the surface to breathe. Often, especially amongst some of the bigger whales, there are seasonal aggregations in very specific areas to give birth. These are effectively an at-sea equivalent of seals' rookeries, or seabird colonies, offering shelter from rough seas and marauding predators, like sharks and orcas.

These aggregations tend to be in warmer waters, and adults often forego feeding for many months in order to migrate and give birth in these areas. Like all young mammals, whales feed on their mother's milk. In whales this in itself is a tricky endeavour, having to suckle underwater involves making an airtight seal around the nipple to get to the fatty, calorie-rich milk.

Longevity

As well as attaining great size, the bigger whales can also live to a great age. Dolphins and porpoises can live to be 20–30 years old; minkes, pilot whales and orcas, about 40–50 years old; sperm whales can live to be 70–80. Fin and blue whales can live to be over 100 years old.

But the record-breaking Methuselah of the whale world is the bowhead whale: in 2007 a harpoon tip last used in the late 19th Century was found embedded in a bowhead whale that had been killed as part of an aboriginal hunt off Alaska. This suggests that the whale was up to 150 years old when it died. Other research on bowheads tentatively suggests they may (if allowed to) attain ages of 200 years. That makes them at least the oldest known mammals in the world, and competitors with Galápagos tortoises and Orange Roughy (a deep-water dwelling fish) for the title of longest-living vertebrate.

Living entirely at sea makes sleep, as we understand it, impossible. Cetaceans do however appear to 'sleep' or rest by effectively shutting down one half of their brain at a time.

Image on facing page:
Humpback mother and calf

To rest of course, means the animals must float at the surface, so they can breathe, and the behaviour of sitting around at the surface not doing very much is called, somewhat aptly, 'logging'.

Communicating

When underwater, external ears are superfluous, and mammalian eyes are of limited use because visibility is often poor, and other animals may be a considerable distance away. Since sound travels much better in water than air, it has become the principal sense for cetaceans. As well as the toothed whales' echolocation to navigate and find prey, whales communicate with each other by creating a variety of sounds.

The most famous is the song of the humpback whales, which is believed to be important in mating rituals. It is the most intricate song of any mammal and can be heard over huge distances. Amazingly, the song seems to evolve and develop over time, but within each specific population of humpbacks the song remains the same – like separate evolving languages.

Dolphins and orcas communicate by high pitched squeaks and whistles, and the sperm whale produces low frequency 'clicking' noises. The loudest whale of all unsurprisingly is the blue whale producing deep loud moaning noises that have been measured to be between 155 and 190 decibels, but way beyond a human's range of hearing. Both blue and fin whales produce these low level sounds to communicate; the noises can travel fantastic distances underwater through canyons and sea troughs for thousands of kilometres, allowing distantly distributed whales to communicate, possibly across entire ocean basins.

The deep sounds of these whales are so pervasive throughout the oceans that they were previously mistaken by scientists to be background noise of the ocean floor creaking!

Place in ecosystem

As some of the largest animals in the oceans, whales interact with the marine ecosystem at different levels. They are predators at various points in the food web; from tiny plankton and crustaceans, all the way up to large fish, squid, mammals, and even other whales. Many species depend on whales too, although they are not always the most photogenic ones – barnacles, whale lice and other parasites have developed close relationships with whales, with many being only found on one particular species. Remoras hitch a ride by clinging to cetaceans, and other fish use the shelter of a big mammal to swim beneath.

This phenomenon is the same one that fishermen exploit by using 'fish aggregation devices' which are basically floating objects that shoaling fish seek shelter beneath.

They also become an essential part of that food web themselves when their carcasses are preyed on by scavengers at sea, including some rather grotesque looking deep water sharks and slimy hagfish. Globally over 400 different species of animals have been recorded on what are euphemistically referred to as 'whale falls' on the ocean floor, where food is scarce and highly prized.

Perhaps most importantly, we should realise that healthy whale populations depend on healthy ocean ecosystems – they are in effect a blubbery biological barometer of the state of our marine environment.

Place in mythology

Whilst early references to dolphins are typically of friendly, beneficial animals, the references to large whales tend to play on the 'monstrous' image. It's not hard to imagine why – uncertain glimpses of enormous beasts – rarely, if ever seen in plain sight. A sinuous hump and a flash of fin or flipper, a gaping mouth, a lunging breach or a towering blow that looked like water or smoke must have been more than enough ammunition to create fantastical beasts, particularly before the advent of opticians. What is clear is that whales do exist in most mythologies of people who were familiar with the seas. Aboriginal people in Australia, North America, Asia and Europe all have their own references to whales; from Jonah's supposed swallowing in the Bible, to the gods and ancestors of Native Americans who existed in orca form. There is also the legend of St. Brendan, an Irish monk born in the late 5th Century AD, who allegedly set foot on an island to say mass, only to find the island was actually a whale. St. Brendan escaped, and centuries later would become known as the patron saint of whales.

But it would be hard today to find anyone who thought of whales as monsters; their cultural position has markedly improved over the centuries – modern day whale references are generally positive, from **Star Trek** to **Finding Nemo**! So let's take a step back to look at how humans and whales have interacted over the years, before we take stock of where our precarious relationship is at today.

EARLY WHALING

2

2 | Early Whaling

First Contact

The earliest known depictions of whales, and whaling, come from rock art at Bangue-Dae in South Korea, dating from around 6000 to 1000BC. Clearly visible are recognisable species of whales, including right, gray and sperm whales, and detailed renditions of hunting them from small boats, using harpoons and air filled bladders attached to ropes.

Other rock carvings from an island off the north coast of Norway represent early whaling taking place there, too, and date from about 2000BC. Oddly enough harpoons were a weapon developed in East Africa some 40,000 years ago, where they were used to hunt aquatic animals like the hippopotamus, the whales' very distant (but closest) cousin.

We don't have a lot of detail about humanity's first interactions with these sea monsters, but it doesn't take much imagination to work out how this is likely to have happened. Early humans were hunter gatherers, making opportunistic uses of food sources as best they could, in the absence of agriculture and supermarkets.

Fresh meat would have been a particular prize, and anything that yielded a lot of it would have been an even bigger prize. Today we regularly hear reports about whales and dolphins getting stuck in harbours, swimming up rivers, or stranding themselves on beaches. Quite often these are already weak, ill, and distressed individuals, but what is clear is that strandings such as these would have occurred in ancient times too.

Image on facing page:
The grim reality of 'the Grind' in the
Faroes, where hundreds of pilot whales
are butchered in shallow water each year

We also know from ancient middens that shellfish were a vital food source to prehistoric shore-dwelling people, so imagine yourself as a primitive human, strolling along the strand line on a beach collecting driftwood to burn, or shellfish to eat, and stumbling across a fresh carcass, or indeed a still-living, stranded whale. It would have been like winning the Neolithic Lottery. A huge source of readily available fresh meat, and the rest of the carcass (bones/teeth/baleen/whatever) to do with as you wanted.

Now, given that such events are quite sporadic, and also at the mercy of favourable winds and tides, this would have been a very boom and bust way to source food. Binge whale eating would have been followed by very lean times, so the jump from passively waiting for the whales and going after them is not a big one. Some species of cetacean are themselves prime candidates for early shore-based persecution. Long-finned pilot whales **(Globicephala melas)** are large members of the dolphin family (up to about 6 metres in length) that are known for being very gregarious.

They travel in large extended family groups of 10–50 (and often many more) and are prone to stranding en masse, and also to getting themselves stuck in shallow bays, fjords and inlets, seemingly disoriented. No one quite knows why this is – as a gregarious species that depends on echolocation, there are several theories, from human-induced noise, changes in the earth's magnetic field, to following inexperienced or distressed family members. Whatever the reason, this behaviour clearly puts them in the firing line for our hungry shore-scouring ancestors.

Driving demand

I've only ever seen pilot whales once in my life, when a small group of them got stuck temporarily in a voe (a bay, or inlet) in Shetland, the most northerly group of islands in Britain. In the 1990s this event drew crowds of onlookers keen to get a glimpse of an animal they would not normally see, but in the past the reaction would have been very different.

In Shetland pilot whales are traditionally called 'the caa'in whale' (caa' means drive) whenever a group of these whales were sighted near shore an opportunistic drive hunt would ensue, with people taking to boats and creating as much noise as possible to herd the whales into voes and shallow water where they could be killed with knives, lances, or whatever weapons were to hand. In the nearby Faroes it is pilot whales that are still driven into fjords and butchered in the 'traditional' drive hunt (which has been going on for centuries), known rather ominously as 'the Grind', which turns the water red with the blood of hundreds of whales every year. Pilot whales also often travel with bigger groups of ocean-going dolphins and have been victim to drive hunts in places like Japan too.

However unpleasant they may be to watch or even imagine, drive hunts are a natural progression for early hunters – corralling their prey into shallow waters so they are trapped and easy to kill. It's just like forcing strandings to happen. But obviously the yields are greater and the whales that are killed are not necessarily just the distressed, ill and disoriented ones.

Another very intriguing method of early whaling was that practised by the hunters of the northwest Pacific, who killed whales by poison. The whales were approached at sea from small boats and stabbed with lances tipped with poison made from aconite, a toxic plant. In what now seems a high risk strategy, they would rely on the stricken animals to be washed back to shore dead by fortuitous winds and currents where they could be retrieved later.

Long-finned pilot whale

Shades of gray

One species of whale has habits that allowed it to become a prime target for early shore whaling, and that is the gray whale (**Eschrichtius robustus**). Hawkeyed readers will perhaps wonder at my spelling of 'gray', and it is a subject for some consideration. I stick to 'gray' with an **A** rather than 'grey' with an **E** because 'gray' is the American English spelling, and since there are no gray whales in the waters around the UK, or indeed Europe or the Atlantic (as a species they are restricted to north Pacific waters) so I personally prefer to respect the Americanized spelling.

But, it was not always thus. Fossil and anecdotal evidence both tell us that there used to be gray whales in the Atlantic too, and not that long ago. Gray whale bones have been found in Sweden, the Netherlands and England, dating from 4000BC to 500AD. So what happened to them?

Gray whales have some somewhat conflicting reputations. They were frequently referred to as 'devilfish' by whalers because of their reputed habit of fiercely defending stricken family members and violently resisting hunters. I'm sure I'm not alone in finding little to chastise gray whales for in such behaviour, but the 'devilfish' name did stick.

The other reputation they have is for being gentle, and

friendly. In some areas they approach boats and seem to actively seek out physical human contact; if you have ever seen a photo of someone leaning out of a boat and kissing or stroking a wild whale, it was probably a gray.

Anyone wishing to imbue whales with some special intelligence would need little persuasion that the different behaviours grays display in response to hunters and benign whale watchers show that they know us better than we think they do. The gray whale is at once a remarkable and unremarkable whale. Yes, it is grey and about 14 metres in length. It's not particularly acrobatic; it has no dorsal fin, but instead a ridge of knobbly 'knuckles' on its back. Its body shows scars and mottled colouration, and its head is covered in callouses, that are also home to parasitic animals like whale lice (which just goes to show, you should be careful where you kiss...). Its throat has between two and four pleats, allowing some expansion, but also marking it out as a baleen whale that's seemingly intermediary between the right whales and the pleat-throated rorquals.

What really marks grays out from other whales is that they are highly migratory shore-huggers. They have evolved to live in shallow coastal waters, and split their time between warm waters and sheltered lagoons for breeding and cold waters for feeding.

They undertake enormous migrations (it's a 20,000 kilometre round trip!) between these two areas, and migrate en masse close to shore on either side of the Pacific Ocean in what are believed to be entirely distinct Eastern and Western populations.

We can only assume it was the same in the Atlantic, where gray whales evidently lived on both sides of the ocean, presumably feeding in the Arctic and breeding and raising their young in more temperate European and American coastal areas. They feed, like other baleen whales, on small invertebrates. But grays exploit a niche no other whales do. They are suction feeders that filter out small shrimp-like crustaceans called amphipods from shallow sandy bottomed waters. Of all the baleen whales, they have the shortest plates, reaching a maximum of about 25cm. Early recollections of these animals often refer to them being amphibious and coming onto land like seals and sea lions do to bask in the sun. These reports are undoubtedly fanciful because although they may be very visible in the extreme shallows, as with other cetaceans, their bulk and blubber would deny them the ability to sun themselves on the beach.

Shore-hugging gray whales were one of the easiest targets for early whalers

But – as an easily accessible coastal species they became prime targets for hunting from the shore. Added to that they had predictable gatherings, by migrating along shore twice a year, and spending months in shallow areas in coastal seas. They were a sitting target for primitive whalers using small boats and hand-held weapons in shallow waters.

We will never really know the true human impact on Atlantic grays; it is lost in the mists of time. And it's possible that they were a species already in trouble from climate change or lack of habitat before we showed up. But we certainly didn't make matters any better. For the true tale of what impact we have had on the shore-hugging grays, we will look later at what has happened to the populations in the Pacific Ocean.

In medieval times, King Alfred had written about whaling in Norway, and the residents of Iceland and France were also said to have a taste for whale meat. Surely opportunistic whaling from shore was happening in other parts of the world too. But the industry of whaling was about to get underway for real in Europe.

From Basques to Corsets
Commercial whaling proper started with one remarkable people, and one very special sort of whale. By the 10th Century the Basque people (of what is now northwestern Spain, and southwestern France) were already well known for hunting whales in the nearby Bay of Biscay.

Using specially built watch towers along the coast, they would set out from shore in small boats to hunt Northern right whales (**Balaena glacialis**), which spent their winter in the balmy waters of the Bay. These are large, rotund whales, up to 18 metres in length, and 100 tonnes in weight. Invariably very dark (almost black) in colour, with no fin, they have huge arched mouths that take up an amazing one quarter of the length of their bodies.

They are recognizable for having pale callosities (rough patches of skin) on their heads, above the eyes, and on upper and lower jaws (analogous to where eyebrows, beards and moustaches would be on a man). These callosities are populated by tightly packed clusters of small crustaceans called whale lice, as well as other animals like barnacles.

They are cold-water specialists, and their rounded shape is due to an amazingly thick layer of blubber, which accounts for about 40% of the whale's body weight. Another area in which the right whales are gifted is their baleen.

Since these species specialise in the smallest prey of any whales – minute plankton called copepods as small as a couple of millimetres in length – they have evolved an amazing array of overlapping baleen plates to filter out these tiny creatures.

The baleen plates of a right whale are typically about 2.5 metres in length, and there are about 600 in an average mouth. With no real predators to fear, these slow moving giants (top speed is only about 9km/h) were conveniently naïve of humans and easy to approach.

Getting it right

The combination of thick blubber, bountiful baleen, predictability, naivety, and the fact that they obligingly float when dead, made right whales the '**right**' whales to catch, hence the imaginative name.

The whalers thought the right whales' convenient attributes were for their own benefit, as illustrated by the recollections of William Scoresby – a second generation whaling captain whose father had made a fortune in Arctic whaling. Young William made his first whaling voyage at the tender age of 11, and was convinced that the tameness and very whaleability of right whales was divine providence: '**the Providence of God is manifested in the tameness and timidity of many of the largest inhabitants of the earth and sea, whereby they fall victims to the prowess of man, and are rendered subservient to his convenience in life. And this was the design of the lower animals in their creation.**'[2] This was clearly wishful thinking on Mr. Scoresby's part, as certainly not all whale species were so apparently willing to fall victim. By the 12th and 13th Centuries the enterprising Basques already had a healthy trade in whale products throughout Europe. They had discovered the value of not the meat from whales but of the blubber and baleen.

Blubber was made into oil for lighting and lubrication, and baleen (commonly called 'whalebone') was used for strengthening and supporting women's petticoats and undergarments, fishing rods, riding whips, and brushes.

As far as meat was concerned, this was cured and exported. Particular value was placed on the massive tongues of the whales, which was considered food fit for royalty.

Perhaps unsurprisingly, as the demand for these whale products grew the local supplies of whales were soon not proving to be enough. It's been suggested that this lack of whales was not down to overexploitation (although that seems to be at the very least a contributory factor) but also down to climatic changes. In any event, the Basques set out first northwards, and then westwards across the Atlantic to look for more lucrative whale fisheries to meet the demand for baleen and oil.

In pursuit of the right whales to catch, they were the first to discover the whales of the cold northwest Atlantic, as well being the first to find the previously untouched stocks of cod **(Gadhus morhua)** which would later support an enormous international fishery.

A precious mouthful: a Southern right
whale shows off its baleen

Arctic whaling

Right whales are a group which also contains the bowhead whale **(Balaena mysticetus)**, which is an Arctic specialist. Bowheads are even larger at up to 20 metres in length and have thicker blubber (often over 50cm thick) and more prodigious baleen (over 700 plates, of up to 4 metres in length) in their enormous mouths. Their lack of a dorsal fin and great bulk allows them to swim under the ice, and they can use their massive head to break through ice up to 30cm thick. They are typically found at the edge of ice sheets though, grazing on their planktonic prey that abounds there. Once their northerly populations were discovered it was soon realized these were an even more right whale to catch.

The Basque monopoly on commercial whaling did not last. With the discovery of Arctic whales stocks in the late 16th Century, English and Dutch ships were soon heading north to pursue whales too. Northern rights, bowheads, and to a lesser extent humpbacks were hunted. By the end of the 16th Century vessels were making regular trips to the Arctic to hunt whales from ports such as Hull on the east coast of England.

Although lucrative, early whaling was a treacherously dangerous and unpleasant job. Whales were approached in small 6-man boats, and a harpoon was thrown at close quarters into the whale. This would not kill it, but attach it by rope to the small boat. Unsurprisingly the unsuspecting whale would usually take flight, attempting to dive or flee to safety, at which point the rope was let out to its full length and the boat would be towed along behind the whale.

Lots of whales would be lost, escaping with or without the harpoon, their fate unknown. After successfully harpooning the animal, it would take at least several hours (and reportedly up to 40 hours!) to exhaust the whale, after which the whalers would take in the rope to get close enough to dispatch the animal by using long lances, stabbing repeatedly to try and puncture the lungs or other vital organs. Many whales probably died as a result of blood loss, exhaustion and stress, as striking fatal blows with lances, at sea, with an unwilling target, (sporting a thick layer of blubber) was a very imperfect process. The floating whale carcass would then be towed back to a shore station on the beach, where the blubber and baleen would be removed. The blubber would be cut up (often using the whales' flukes as a chopping board) and boiled in large pots called 'try-works' for several hours to render it to oil. The oil was then put into barrels and returned to the ship.

Although the tongues were taken for meat, it seems that by now whalers largely left the rest of the carcass to waste. Oil and baleen were the lucrative commodities sought by the Arctic whalers, and that was what they wanted to fill their hold with. Whale oil was now routinely burned in streetlamps and homes to provide light, and was also used in the manufacture of wool and leather.

The precious baleen commanded an even greater price, its tough yet malleable qualities being much in demand for an amazing array of products, most famously the corsets and supports for women's skirts. In hot water the baleen became pliant and could be shaped however it was required, drying to a hardened, rigid shape: the product of the big blubbery whales helping to give women fashionably waspish waists.

A New England

Limited good whaling grounds and suitable shore sites meant that competition was already fierce between Dutch and English whalers. Whaling became big business, and serious politics. English and Dutch whalers were escorted by armed naval vessels to claim the blubbery riches of the Arctic for their own. To gain advantage through whaling experience, their vessels often had Basque whalers as part of the crew.

The demand for baleen and blubber grew, as whale oil was now used for making soap, textiles and in other manufacturing industries, and baleen was in vogue for the fashion trade and a myriad of other uses. At the same time shore-based whaling was beginning on a bigger scale in the new North American colonies, with the now seemingly improbable location of Long Island, New York being the centre of the American east coast's shore whaling industry.

Renewed effort in the 18th and 19th Centuries saw a second phase of British whaling in the Arctic, with ports from all round Britain sending fleets northwards. Ultimately the east coast ports prospered, with some of them building up a crucial dependence on the northern whaling industry.

Hull, Dundee, Peterhead, etc. all had thriving industries sending boats up to the Arctic. It was an unpleasant business, with ships and crew often being lost in the ice, but a profitable one. Early whalers also hunted whatever else they could find of value in the frozen north. Seals, walrus, foxes and polar bears were routinely hunted, with pelts and tusks being brought back to trade. Other species such as great auks were used to supplement onboard food rations too.

As was to become the pattern, whaling catches diminished in the Arctic whaling grounds, and the discovery of a new, more profitable species of whale to target was to see New England replace old England and Holland as the centre of the whaling world.

3

THERE ONCE WAS A WHALE FROM NANTUCKET...

3 | There once was a whale from Nantucket ...

The whale of a time

Legend has it that the island of Nantucket was created when a giant emptied sand out of his shoe. The neighbouring Martha's Vineyard was supposed to have been the other shoeful. Sitting below the outstretched arm of Cape Cod, in the Eastern US state of Massachusetts, Nantucket is the island that launched dozens of bawdy limericks and a global whaling industry targeting the sperm whale.

Nantucket today is a quiet, genteel place that attracts a steady stream of tourists, and those seeking some peace and quiet. However in its hey-day it was the centre of commercial whaling worldwide and traded directly with London to supply whale oil to light fashionable drawing rooms. In fact two of the three ships involved in the famous 'Boston Tea Party' incident (where their cargos of tea from London were thrown overboard, in protest at the undercutting of local merchants) had been carrying whale oil from Nantucket on their previous voyage.

I can remember looking out from the roof of the Nantucket whaling museum, housed in a converted candle factory, over the vista of Nantucket town. The wide sweeping arc of a harbour, picturesque lighthouses, spotlessly-maintained clapboard houses and cobbled streets suggest a place that either hasn't quite caught up with the present day, or doesn't want to. Above your head, the weather vane of an arching sperm whale reminds you of the island's history of involvement with that very special species.

Image on facing page:
The roof of the Nantucket whaling museum,
featuring the whale that defined the island

If ever a town was built on the foundations of whale bones, this is it. Nantucketers, like everyone else in New England, conducted shore whaling for species like rights, humpbacks, and whatever else they could get. But as a small island on the periphery of the new colonies, they were nothing special. Nantucket shore whaling had started properly in the late 1660s when a whale, probably a sickly right whale, became trapped in the harbour and the locals took to boats to finish it off. But it was another couple of fortunate accidents that were to send Nantucket whalers around the world to chase the sperm whale. In about 1700 a sperm whale had stranded on a Nantucket beach, and it was found to yield oil of amazing quality. The sperm whale oil's main advantage was its waxy quality: three quarters of it made up of waxy fatty acids, which could be separated to create a dry, brittle wax (which they called 'pure spermaceti') that was perfect for making candles.

Then the story goes that in 1712 a shore whaling boat was blown offshore into a pod of sperm whales some distance out to sea from Nantucket. Somehow, they managed to kill one and tow it back to shore. Never before had people known where to seek these beasts, or that there were substantial numbers of them for the taking, and very quickly Nantucket developed a whaling industry that would set sail in search of the whale that would be their fortune. Nantucket's geographical position now made it the ideal base for a whaling industry with its sight set to the high seas. The town itself grew to accommodate and exploit the trappings of the whaling industry.

Boat builders, traders, oil and candle factories, and all manner of supporting industries developed. At its peak the small island of Nantucket was seen as the epicentre of whaling expertise and would have a fleet of around 90 whaling ships. A man was not a man in Nantucket until he had killed a whale or rounded Cape Horn.

Deeply odd

The sperm whale (**Physeter macrocephalus**) is not like any of the other great whales. For a start it's the only great whale that has teeth, it's also the only toothed whale that has attained a truly enormous size. Being a toothed whale, it has only one blowhole, rather strangely situated on the left at the very front of its oddly oblong head. The shape of the head (which accounts for one third of the animal) is perhaps the most remarkable feature of a sperm whale. If you look at a skeleton, such as the one that dominates the Nantucket whaling museum's main room, then the noticeable difference is the lack of baleen, and the possession of a lower jaw studded with large teeth, but this alone does not account for the strange profile.

The sperm whale possesses a cavity in its forehead that is called the 'spermaceti' organ. This literally translates as 'whale seed', as the creamy, waxy liquid in the spermaceti organ was believed to be just that. Of course, it isn't.

To this day we do not definitively know what the spermaceti is for – theories abound, including some role in echolocation, as the 'forehead' is the area in other toothed whales that is used for echolocation; some way of helping regulate buoyancy and deal with extreme pressures when taking deep dives, and a shock absorber to allow the whale to behave like a living battering ram.

And when I say deep dives, I mean deep. The sperm whale holds the record for the deepest diving mammal – reaching known depths of over 2 kilometres.

This deep diving whale routinely stays underwater for over an hour between breaths, and is believed to be able to stay down for up to two hours. They mostly eat squid, but also eat fish, and it is probably largely this squid-dominated diet that gives sperm whale oil different properties from other great whales.

The toothy lower jaw is believed to be of more use for fighting than for feeding and being a toothed whale, the males, or 'bulls', are considerably bigger and toothier than the females.

Giant squid

Adult bulls can reach 18 metres, although tales of momentous encounters at sea suggest that before intense exploitation there were bigger beasts out there. Indeed, the Nantucket whaling museum has on display a 5.5 metre lower jaw bone. The proportions of the jaw bone suggests its owner was a whopping 28 metres or so long when alive (which would make them almost as big as today's blue whale).

Sperm whales also have the largest brain of any animal that has ever lived, weighing in at an impressive 7.8 kilograms, as well as the largest skull of any whale, and the thickest skin of any animal (at about 36cm). They have an undeniable place in literary history as the archetypal monstrous whale in **Moby Dick**, and **Pinocchio**. If anyone ever was truly swallowed by a whale – it could only have been a sperm whale.

On my desk is a scale-model (that sounds so much more defensible than 'toy') of a sperm whale. It is wrapped in an enraged embrace with a similarly-scaled giant squid. Whilst our images of this titanic battle of deep-sea denizens may be solely from film, TV, and illustration, we nonetheless know they happen.

At up to 18 metres in length, the giant squid is one of the biggest invertebrates that has ever lived (it has a bigger cousin, the aptly named colossal squid, who is even more formidable, and less well understood), yet we know very, very little about them. It was only in 2005 that a live adult giant squid was caught on camera for the first time.[3] What we do know is that scars and

undigested remains show us that sperm whales frequently battle with and eat giant squid. Many, if not most, of the rare giant squid remains that have been studied have come from the stomachs of dead sperm whales. Most of the squid these whales eat are however much smaller species, at about a metre or two in length.

The horny beaks of squid cause irritation in the sperm whales' digestive system – leading it to secrete an odd substance called ambergris. This literally translates as 'grey amber' and was known since ancient times as a valuable commodity. Given its unsavoury intestinal origins, it is somewhat gratifying to know that the principal for which ambergris gained demand in previous centuries was for making perfume. It was a rare and unusual commodity, quite literally, worth its weight in gold.

Sperm whales, unlike rights and grays, prefer warmer waters. They do not have predictable migratory patterns, or thick layers of blubber, and are almost always found in offshore, deep waters, or the edges of continental shelves, where they often congregate in large numbers.

They are a formidable adversary, both when defending their young and having harpoons hurled at them, and so it is not for nothing that they have been immortalised as fearsome 'monsters'. But the quality of clear-burning oil, the added spermaceti (which, it is claimed, made the finest candles ever), and ambergris made sperm whales well worth the hunt.

The Nantucket whalers headed north out to sea, and

south to warmer waters to seek their new prey, and whaling trips changed from small shore-based operations to lengthy sea-going journeys. Vessels got bigger, trips got longer, and the whales usually needed to be processed alongside and on the ships. In effect, these whaling ships would become prototype factory ships, catching and processing animals at sea. It was a messy, dangerous job, but at least they didn't have to brave the treacherous polar ice, even if they were faced with a much fiercer quarry.

Going the distance

As whales were increasingly hunted out of more easily reachable grounds, the trips became longer and longer – and as the qualities of the superior oils became known, demand increased too. Soon, spermaceti candles were lighting all the best homes and Nantucket was doing a roaring trade directly with London.

Nantucket was thriving, and the New England whaling industry was booming. Whenever whales became scarce (as they inevitably did) they travelled further still, to the Azores, through equatorial waters, and to the South Atlantic. Then in 1789 whalers aboard the **Emilia**, an English vessel crewed by Nantucket whalemen, rounded Cape Horn and found an entire ocean full of unexploited whales in the Pacific.

The Pacific Ocean was an untapped sea of plenty. Quickly whaling fleets moved to exploit the blubbery bounty of right, humpback and especially sperm whales that abounded in these waters. Soon whalers were taking an estimated 8,000–10,000 whales per year. New England's whaling trips went from months to years, and by turn of the 19th Century the average length of a whaling trip was three or even four years long. Whaling was now a more efficient process, with the advent of onboard try-works the spermaceti and blubber could be processed more quickly (in tropical climates it had to be, to stop it spoiling in the heat, and rendering the entire catch worthless), and at sea.

That necessitated a very messy process whereby the dead whales were tied alongside the vessel and processed there from a platform made of narrow wooden planks, using cutting blades mounted on 5 metre poles. Usually the blubber was cut off in one spiralling, continuous strip, like a bigger and more macabre satsuma peel. The whaling crews had to fend off hordes of sharks attracted to the bloody carcass, snatching mouthfuls of blubber. Crewmen also needed to take care not to fall, or be knocked into the water amongst the scavengers themselves, despite the boat's deck being slick with blood, oil and water.

The sperm whale's oddly oblong forehead contained valuable spermaceti, and made a formidable battering ram

Perhaps the grimmest job of all was usually allocated to the smallest, youngest crew member, and involved climbing inside the head of the sperm whale to scoop out the valuable spermaceti into a bucket. Once everything of value had been stripped from the whale, the remains of the carcass would be discarded to the hordes of waiting scavengers. Of course these jobs were made all the more dangerous in bad weather or stormy seas.

Dangerous at both ends

Harpooning the animals was still done by small boats, although now they would quite often try to have more than one boat attached fast to the animal to try to exhaust it. It was an even more dangerous job with sperm whales than with right whales, and the gruelling experience of hanging on whilst the stricken whale exhausted itself and tried to free itself from the harpoon came to be known as the 'Nantucket sleighride', despite the 30km/h test of endurance having few of the cosy, pleasurable trappings that the word 'sleighride' evokes.

Given its well-armed lower jaw, as well as the forceful fluke, both ends of the sperm whale were equally feared at close quarters. Many crew men were lost to whales furiously fighting the harpoons and lances of the whalers. Even greater tragedy was to face two whaling ships, the **Essex** and the **Ann Alexander**, which both sank after being rammed by enraged bull sperm whales. It was the tale of the **Essex** which inspired Herman Melville's **Moby Dick**, although the true story varies from the literary one.

The whale that struck the **Essex** was estimated to be some 26 metres long, and only eight out of twenty crew members survived the ordeal and being subsequently stranded at sea without provisions, some of them having to resort to cannibalism of their dead crew mates to survive.

Traversing the Pacific meant discovering new lands, and making more stops for provisions too. New ports grew up to serve the burgeoning industry. San Francisco on the American west coast became a bustling whale port, taking advantage of the Pacific Ocean on its doorstep.

As well-known areas became increasingly devoid of large numbers of targetable whales, sights were set elsewhere. The new colonies of New Zealand, South Africa and Australia offered rich whaling grounds for (Southern) rights, humpbacks and sperm whales.

Go West

Off the western coast of North America lay an untouched wealth of whales. The Eastern Pacific population of gray whales (commonly known as 'Californian grays') undertook their mammoth 10,000 kilometre migration twice a year along the western seaboard. In one of the most momentous of all cetacean journeys, they split their time between the cold Arctic feeding grounds and the warm waters of the Gulf of California where they calved and nursed their young in shallow lagoons, congregating in large groups, the location offering protection from rough seas, and the sheer numbers of whales offering a safeguard against predators that would target whale calves.

These predictable and accessible congregations made grays easy targets, once the calving lagoons were discovered by Charles Scammon in 1856. Despite the whales being relatively poor in yielding oil, being able to catch them in large numbers was well worth the whalers' effort. Whalers would kill every whale they could, and even ruthlessly exploit the bond between mother and calf by targeting the calves to make the adult whales come closer out of concern for their young. Whilst it now seems abhorrent that they were hunted en masse as they took shelter to give birth and nurse their young, at the time it was seen as just a convenient opportunity.

The Californian gray rush was to prove a time-limited opportunity. Unsurprisingly, concerted persecution of the species in their breeding grounds had a devastating effect. Over 8,000 gray whales had been hunted by the 1870s, and the stocks had crashed so much that the population of Californian grays was on the brink of extinction.

In fact, this population of whales was to go on to be presumed extinct twice. In the first instance, as soon as some remaining whales were found (despite assuming they had hunted them to the point of extirpation) they too were immediately targeted by whalers.

The end is nigh?

Around the world the populations of reachable, huntable whales were all following the same pattern of excited discovery, followed by rampant whaling, followed by stock decline. Sperm whales, right whales, bowheads, grays and humpbacks had been exploited to the best of the whalers' ability. But, alongside declining catches, the discovery of oil in Pennsylvania in 1859 was to strike a serious blow against the whaling industry. This seemed to offer a more stable and dependable source of fuel oil, and diminishing returns were making whaling unprofitable.

For a brief time it seemed that the discovery of black gold would mean an end to the persecution of blubbery gold.

In all the centuries of whaling so far, the whales targeted had been taken because they were possible to hunt. They could be approached and hunted from small vessels, and they floated when they died. There were however oceans full of other whales that had never been targeted – the lean, fast rorquals. Too fast to hunt from small rowboats, they were streamlined whales that had lower amounts of blubber, so they also sank when dead. All in all they were not a good target for early whalers. But timely technological advances in the late 19th Century meant that the unsuspecting rorquals were now also in the whalers' firing line.

4

The tail end of the biggest animal ever
known to have lived – the blue whale

4 | Systematic cetacean annihilation

Meet the Rorquals

Six of the ten species of Great whales are rorquals, namely: blue, fin humpback, sei, Bryde's and minke. With the slightly odd exception of the humpback, they all follow the same basic body plan, but vary in size.

They are streamlined, lean whales with pleated throats (the Norwegian name for which gives us the name 'rorqual') that allow them to expand their throat greatly and gulp feed big mouthfuls of food similar to a pelican's beak, which they usually do whilst near or at the surface. Let's get quickly acquainted with them all, starting within the biggest, the daddy of all vertebrates, the blue whale.

At up to 30 metres long (and possibly even longer), an adult blue whale (**Balaenoptera musculus**) is truly gigantic. It is longer than a diplodocus, weighs 190 tonnes – equivalent to the weight of about 1,500 people – and can eat 3,600 kilograms of food in a day. The blow of a blue whale can easily reach over 9 metres in height, or three storeys high. Blue whales are so rarely encountered these days that there are still huge gaps in our knowledge about them, with the exception of a relatively well-studied population off the Californian coast. For example, we still don't know where the biggest animals on the planet go to breed, let alone have an understanding of their social structures or population dynamics.

Famously, blue whales predominantly feed on large plankton, and in particular a small crustacean called krill. Krill are small free-swimming shrimp-like animals that are only a few centimetres long at most. They are found in cold and temperate waters, where they can form massive swarms. The humble krill form the basis of the entire Antarctic food web.

Fin whales (**Balaenoptera physalus**) at up to 27 metres long are only slightly smaller than blues, and have distinctive asymmetrical colouration, which is even visible in their baleen. I think that maybe the distinctive chevrons behind the fin whale's head act as go-faster stripes, as they are the swiftest of all the great whales easily reaching speeds of 30km/h, which, along with their streamlined shape earns them one of their nicknames, as 'greyhound of the ocean'. Fin whales are widespread, and found in oceans all over the world, but tend to prefer colder or more temperate waters. They are opportunistic feeders, often feeding on small shoaling fish like herring by spectacularly 'lunge-feeding' at the ocean surface.

We shall meet the engaging humpbacks **(Megaptera novaeangliae)** in some more detail later on, but they are the odd ones in the rorqual family, which is why they have been placed in a separate genus; the name **Megaptera** meaning 'giant wings', referring to their vast pectoral fins. They are also much plumper than the other rorquals, with thicker blubber, and were an easier target for early whalers by their convenient buoyancy when dead. Amongst all the great whales they are arguably the most photogenic and entertaining. At a maximum size of about 17 metres, and weighing in at 35 tonnes, they would need about 5 adult African elephants to balance them on a (well-reinforced) see-saw.

Sei whales **(Balaenoptera borealis)** are a similar length to humpbacks, but much more slender. They usually feed at the surface on their preferred food which is krill and plankton. They tend to avoid the very coldest waters, and are amongst the least predictable of the great whales to locate.

Bryde's whales **(Balaenoptera edeni)** are warm water rorquals, the only one of the group not to be found in the Southern Ocean feeding grounds. They can be as big as sei whales, but are often considerably smaller, with adults being as short as 10 metres in length. They predominantly eat small fish, and are named after the man who set up the first whaling factory in South Africa.

The minke whale **(Balaenoptera acutrostrata)** is reportedly so-called because of an amusing story about an overexaggerating whaler. As the smallest of the rorquals, up to a maximum of 11 metres in length and often sporting distinctive white 'armband' markings, they gained their name from an infamous Norwegian whaler (called Meincke) who was renowned for grossly overestimating the size of the whales he'd seen. It became commonplace to mockingly refer to small whales as 'Meincke's whales', which in turn became simply 'minkes'. A competing story is that the name comes from a Norwegian word meaning to get increasingly smaller. They are temperate water whales, with separate populations in northern and southern hemispheres and exist in relatively larger numbers than the bigger whales for two very good reasons. Firstly, smaller animals are generally more numerous than big ones, that's the way nature works. Secondly, minkes were not targeted by whalers effectively until all of the bigger whales had been reduced severely in numbers. As small whales, they just weren't seen to be worth the effort.

Modern whaling
With the decline in easy to hunt species of whales (the slow, floating ones) attention fell to the swifter whales that were regularly seen by whalers but had previously been too fast to catch. As well as the depleted stocks of the other whales, there were two crucial technological advances that put rorquals in the whalers' firing line: faster, steam-powered vessels, and explosive harpoons. With this armoury, the stage was set for the late 19th and 20th Centuries to witness the greatest ever levels of whaling, which could now reach every corner of the globe – no whale populations were to be safe.

Svend Foyn, a Norwegian sealer, is considered to be the father of modern whaling, having been the first to combine the efficiency of steam-powered ships and explosive harpoons, which led to a resurgence in whaling initially in the North Atlantic at the turn of the 20th Century. Foyn developed a bow-mounted swiveling harpoon-gun, using a one-metre harpoon with a grenade at its tip, which exploded when it penetrated the whale's

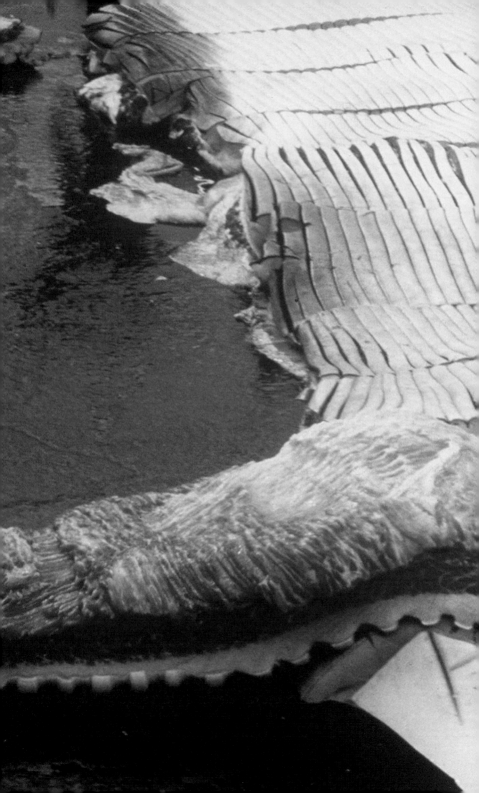

body, its insides being shot through with shrapnel. The new 1 tonne harpoon gun had a range of some 40 metres, and was robust enough to absorb the recoil. This was then winched back to the ship using steam power. Grenade-tipped harpoons fired from the prow of a ship are still the principal method of hunting great whales to this day.

In 1863 Foyn first used this new technology to kill a blue whale – now even the biggest of species was within reach. The previously unattainable rorqual species were now hunted remorselessly. Shore stations were established in the North Atlantic islands of Shetland, Orkney, the Faroes and the Hebrides to exploit the surrounding seas. These stations provided sites where big whales could be hauled ashore and processed.

Hunting rorquals needed additional new techniques as well, because, with the humpback exception, rorquals are quite lean whales, with small layers of blubber. That means they unhelpfully sink when dead. Hunting rorquals therefore needed advances in winching technology, to allow for the great strain of a sinking whale and also a way of inflating the carcasses with air to make them float and be able to be towed back to shore. It also means that there is less oil from the blubber – but it was soon found that the whale flesh too contained oil, and could be rendered down to produce it. It strikes us now as a remarkably wasteful exercise, given that the meat was effectively being wasted, but there was very little market or appetite for whalemeat, even amongst those who hunted them. The initial targets of the whalers were the bigger whales – who clearly delivered more buck for their bang.

Image on preceding page:
A fin whale being 'flensed' – blubber being cut from the flesh into strips

North Atlantic whaling

Island communities proved to be ideally situated for shore whaling stations, exploiting the surrounding seas. The islanders themselves though were often surprisingly hostile to the processing facilities. For the most part their reservations may have been economic, as in the case of Shetland, the stations were Norwegian-owned and operated, meaning the local folk got little of the benefits. There was also concern from islanders even then that the whaling industry was causing damage to the ecosystem (albeit they seemed to be most concerned with the possible effects on the local herring fishery, blaming the shore stations for decreasing catches!)

In the first few years of the 20th Century Shetland would see three whaling stations established there, two in the far north, at Rona's Voe, and one in the centre of the mainland at Olna Firth. It's hard to imagine them now; both places are very quiet. Rona's Voe – dominated by the austere red sandstone slopes of Shetland's highest hill – is very remote, even by Shetland standards, and the little peaceful village of Voe on Olna Firth certainly doesn't conjure up images of a bloody industry rendering thousands of whales to make oil. The station at Olna is significant as it was an early part of the business of Salvesens, which would go on to be the single biggest whaling company in the world.

The early days of modern whaling yielded huge numbers of whales in the North Atlantic. I find the numbers startling, as someone who's lived in Shetland and been around Scotland and the North Sea a bit, it's clear that these waters today aren't exactly teeming with cetaceans – and the reason for that is probably that most of the larger ones were fished out. These days it seems that species like humpbacks are making a comeback in these seas, being more frequently sighted – but they are still rare enough to make such sightings newsworthy. Between 1908 and 1914, 2,413 fin whales, and 1,283 sei whales were caught within Scottish fisheries districts alone.[4] In 1924 Olna whaling station saw its peak year with 448 whales caught and landed, some 352 of them fins. Unsurprisingly, the reachable whales in the waters around the whaling stations became increasingly depleted of whales. As the whales in the North Atlantic became increasingly hard to find, the attention of the Norwegian companies was heading southwards.

Migrating south

'Modern' whaling had by now spread elsewhere too, particularly targeting whales in the North Pacific. New technology (with faster ships and deadlier ammunition) meant too that the remaining Arctic whales that had so far eluded the whaling effort there were now possible to catch. But there was still one vast, untapped population of whales previously out of reach, physically and economically unviable to pursue. The whalers of the North Atlantic would literally have to go to the ends of the earth as sights shifted to the whale populations in the Southern Ocean. 1892 saw the first tentative whaling voyage to the Antarctic.

As a rule, the rorqual whales split their time between feeding and breeding. This often entails lengthy migrations between the two areas, and also means that for considerable time each year the whales are unable to feed. Breeding and calving tends to happen in warmer, more tropical waters which are relatively poor for prey species, but provide more safety from predators. Feeding tends to take place in colder, more nutrient-rich waters at higher latitudes, which offer less protection for young calves, but more food for hungry adults. Nowhere was this more evident than in the Southern Ocean. Vast numbers of different species of baleen whales spent the southern summer gorging on the productive cold waters off Antarctica, principally feeding on the enormous swarms of krill that form the basis of the Southern Ocean's food web.

Given that the rorqual whales were being hunted essentially just for oil, there was also another consideration that made targeting them in colder feeding grounds more logical: when breeding in warmer seas whales lose vast quantities of fat reserves, due to the exertions of migrating to and from the calving grounds, giving birth, and feeding newly-born young.

Clearly not only is blubber an effective insulator, it is also an essential fuel tank, storing energy for leaner times. The return trips to the feeding grounds use up the last of the whales' reserves of energy. By the time they return to the feeding grounds in colder waters, they are emaciated and ravenous. It made sense for whalers to target whales where their concentrations were greatest, and also when they had the most profitable fatty physiques.

We're gonna need a bigger boat

Whaling in the Antarctic was no small undertaking; it is the most inhospitable ocean on earth, and half a world away from the North Atlantic. In order to get there whalers needed big vessels, and somewhere to process the whales. Shore whaling stations were needed, where the massive rorquals could be winched on land and processed. Early stations at South Georgia and South Shetland Islands were built, which could accommodate hundreds of men, and provide bases for processing whales caught at sea and towed back.

Men from across Britain, including many who had previous experience of whaling in the North Atlantic sailed with the Norwegian-owned companies to the Antarctic. It was a hard life, with journeys typically lasting a full year. As with other lengthy seafaring journeys, they took advantage of what other natural abundance they found, thinking nothing of using native birds for eggs, killing walruses and seals for food, and even collecting penguins for zoo collections. Although it seems like an unlikely occupation, given the exceptional distances involved and disruption to home life, whaling in the Antarctic offered an opportunity to many – particularly for those in places like the Northern Isles of Scotland, who were facing hard times. Many without work may have been forced to emigrate were it not for the relatively lucrative whaling jobs. Initially the whaling in the Southern Ocean was dominated by Norwegian and British vessels, often relying on the combination of British investment and Norwegian labour. Salvesens were based at Leith, near

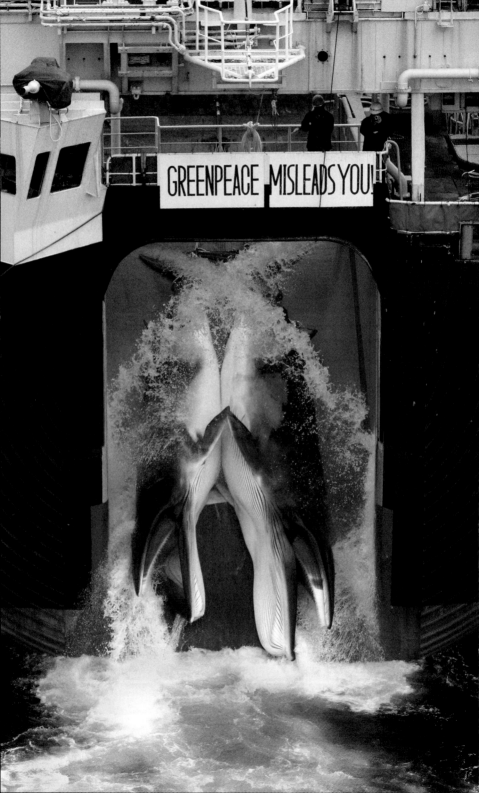

Edinburgh in Scotland, and they even named their new whaling station in the Falkland Islands 'Leith Harbour' after the old town. This initial Antarctic whaling effort focussed on the plentiful humpbacks and also Southern right whales **(Balaena australis)** that abounded in the seas around the whaling stations. In a by now familiar pattern, it was not long until the whale numbers locally had dwindled. By the start of World War I, some 19 whaling firms were whaling in the Antarctic. Soon Norway and Britain would be exploiting the Southern Ocean's whales equally, as British involvement in whaling increased.

More than 18,000 humpback whales were killed in the decade after the establishment of whaling stations in South Georgia. In a matter of only a few years the plentiful whales around each of the whaling stations were less easy to find, and whale catching vessels had to travel further to find their prey. With this in mind a solution to the high costs and geographical ties of the whaling stations was needed – and a solution came in the ominous form of a factory whaling vessel.

Factored out

Even without factory ships, Antarctic whaling had started to take its toll on the bigger rorquals. Salvesens recorded having caught 3,064 whales in the 1915–16 season. Of these over half (1,701) were blues, and 800 were fins. The arrival of factory ships would only increase the threat to these, the biggest of whales. The first factory ship, the **Lancing**, sailed for the Southern Ocean in 1925. In 1926 the **C.F. Larsen** was fitted out, at 13,246 tonnes.5 It was at the time the biggest ship ever to be part of a whaling fleet. Designed to be floating processing stations, these ships had a stern ramp big enough to winch a blue whale up – whales could now be processed onboard and at sea with ruthlessly remarkable speed.

Image on facing page:
Two minke whales are hauled aboard the stern
ramp of a modern day factory whaling ship

By the 1930s Norway, Britain, the Netherlands, USA, South Africa and the USSR all had their own fleets operating in the whale-rich waters around Antarctica. For the first time large whales could be caught, transferred to the factory ship, towed up the ramp at the rear and processed on deck. It marked a new era in whaling – the whalers could now follow the whales wherever they were, which is just what they did. In the late 1930s they were joined by Japanese and German fleets keen to help plunder the wealth of the whale-rich waters. By 1938, 92% of the world's whale oil was coming from the Antarctic.

With the advent of the factory ships a new, phenomenally big, prize was up for grabs. Blue whales could be properly targeted in the Southern Ocean for the first time, without the restriction of being limited to whales in the proximity of shore stations. The factory ships could target the whales wherever they were, and they were targeted relentlessly. Because it took the same effort to hunt and kill a whale regardless of species, it made sense to target the biggest animals to get the most reward.

The focus was therefore initially blue, and to a lesser extent fin, whales. In the 1930–31 season over 40,000 whales were killed in the Southern Ocean – three-quarters of them blue whales. In another twist of unsustainability, the larger rorqual whales of each species tended to be females, which because of their need to carry and care for young are considerably bigger than males. And the majority of those females, whilst feeding in the Southern Ocean, would be pregnant.

Margarine and munitions

In the 1930s diesel engines were adopted by the whaling fleets. These noisier vessels meant that harpooning whales involved chasing and exhausting the whales until they were within range. Over the following years, newer, bigger factory fleets chased ever smaller numbers of whales. As the big blues became more difficult to find, attention shifted to fins, and then on down the size scale. New demands for whale oil meant more competition. Oil was now increasingly desirable for food. As well as the

Japanese taste for whalemeat driving its own fleets south, the scientific breakthrough of the turn of the 20th Century meant it was now possible to hydrogenate oil into fat, in particular for margarine. Global demand for edible fats made whaling once again a lucrative business. As well as using whales to light your lamps, and lubricate your machinery, you could now smear them on your face and spread them on your sandwiches. As if that wasn't enough, a by-product was glycerine, which went on to be in great demand for manufacturing explosives.

The 'waste' of whale meat continued apace; despite attempts to market it to the UK public, there was little appetite. Japan solely seemed to have a market for eating whale meat, as they had done with shore-caught whales caught in coastal regions for centuries. Surplus whale meat was ground up for animal feeds and fertilisers, but this was always only a small sideline of the operation. It was all about the oil. The baleen, which had been such a valued prize in previous decades, was now discarded as cheaper synthetic alternatives were available.

Aboard a factory ship a massive blue whale could be processed onboard in only one hour, about the time it takes to get some photos developed. At its peak in the 1937–38 season, global whaling was to kill approximately 55,000 whales.

Industrial whaling: SO last century
With diminishing returns, the whalers knew that there was a problem, and they were also fully aware that it was all down to overhunting. But as with most maritime overexploitation, it's always easier to blame everyone else, and then just redouble your own efforts to grab what you can. In his book **The Unnatural History of the Sea**, which charts centuries of human exploitation of the oceans, Professor Callum Roberts described whaling as **'the first truly global industry'**.[6] It's also the best and worst example of the 'Tragedy of the Commons', namely that when a shared resource is open to exploitation from a number of individuals, it always becomes depleted, because the most sensible option for each competing party is to take more

than their fair share. Everyone wanted a piece of the action, and everyone wanted as much profit as they could get.

The concern was not for the whales, or what was being done to them, their populations, and their ecosystem. In the cold, harsh world of the Southern Ocean, it was cold hard cash that mattered. So even when the whalers began to realise the scale of the problem, and just how unsustainable the levels of whaling were, the hunting continued apace.

As early as 1912 concerns were being voiced directly at those prosecuting the 'southern whale fishery'. Theodore Salvesen gave a lecture to the Royal Society of Arts in London about the wondrous advances in 20th Century whaling, enabling the pursuit of whales in the Antarctic. An audience member, who had himself been a whaler in the Arctic, told him that if they were already getting so many whales, it would not be long before the fishery floundered and **'the whales would practically disappear from the sea'.**[7]

Blue whale

The catch of whales in a single year in the early 20th Century was equivalent to an entire decade's worth of American high seas whaling of the previous century. Global whaling had increased ten-fold.

It was no Damascean conversion that stopped most countries from whaling; it was the economic reality of diminishing returns, and the increasing availability of cheaper alternatives to whale products. The world was moving on, and the production of synthetic alternatives to whale bone, and cheaper sources of oil from nuts, vegetables and other crops were making the industry increasingly unprofitable.

In the end there simply wouldn't be enough whales left to make it worth their while.

5

Killed whales are tied alongside
the catcher boats until they can
be transferred to the factory ship
for processing

5 | Regulation, Regulation, Regulation

All at sea

True modern pelagic (at-sea) whaling only really began in 1925 and by 1928 the global catch of whales was almost 24,000 animals. Until then the focus of Southern Ocean whaling stations in South Georgia and the like had been on locally-available whales like humpbacks that were towed back to the shore stations to be rendered into barrels of oil. Unsurprisingly, the local humpback numbers soon dwindled around the whaling stations, and it was the development of factory ships that allowed an enormous expansion in whaling effort, and resulted in a disaster for the world's whales.

Norway and Britain were now the world's dominant whaling nations, and faced with a slump in the global oil price and emerging concerns over the sustainability of the industry, they reached a bilateral agreement to voluntarily restrict their whaling operations from between the years of 1932 and 1937. These early concerns were more about offering stability to the industry than any regard for what was happening to whales.

Internationally, the whaling nations seemed to be starting to realise that there was a problem, and tentative steps were taken to try to regulate the industry, for their shared good. In 1931 an International Convention for the Regulation of Whaling was approved by 26 nations at the Assembly of the League of Nations, but this had very little effect.

First steps of regulating whaling

It wasn't until 1937 that the first International Whaling Convention met, in London. The signatories to it were: Great Britain, Norway, USA, Australia, New Zealand, Germany, the Argentine Republic, the Union of South Africa and Ireland. The convention agreed to three conditions. Firstly, to limit the whaling season in the Southern Ocean (between 8th December and 7th March). Number two: set minimum size limits for animals by whale species (e.g. blues must be longer than 21 metres, humpbacks longer than 10.5 metres). And thirdly, give full protection to already depleted stocks, such as right and gray whales.

Given that all of the participating nations agreed this, it seems on paper to be very much a step in the right direction. But irrespective of the decisions, five whaling expeditions (four Japanese and one South African) were to continue whaling without any consideration for the agreed limits. International agreements on whaling seem to have been flouted from the very beginning.

The following year saw the Convention's agreement renewed, with some modifications to restrict whaling further. To better protect depleted stocks of humpbacks it was forbidden to hunt them south of 40 degrees South. And the first internationally agreed whale sanctuary was set between longitudes 70 degrees E and 70 degrees W in the Southern Ocean. Despite attempts by Norway to fix a limit on the number of whaling vessels, there were crucially no restrictions made on the numbers of boats involved or whaling capacity.

Again, this looks on paper like things were moving (albeit slowly) in the right direction, but 1937–38 was to become the season when global whale catches reached what would be their peak, with a staggering 54,835 whales being killed, 84% of them in the Antarctic.

Japan had joined the pelagic whale-pillaging club in 1930s when they sent their own factory ships to the Southern Ocean. By the end of the 1930s Japan and Germany accounted for about 30% of the total global catch of whales, both countries having swiftly increased their whaling efforts in the Southern Ocean in the period between world wars.

The Conference met again in 1939, and five nations (Great Britain, Norway, Germany, Japan and Norway) renewed the previous agreement with some detailed changes. Twenty-eight factory vessels set sail for the 1939–40 season (10 Norwegian, 10 British, 6 Japanese, 1 Panamanian and 1 American).

Then World War II began. The war gave the Antarctic whales some respite from the factory ships that conferences and agreements had not been able to. There was no pelagic whaling between 1941 and 1943. Busy pointing weapons at each other, the main whaling nations were too preoccupied to point harpoons at whales, and the factory ships were recruited to the war effort, to be used as oil tankers. The big whaling factory ships seemed to prove to be easy targets, and of the 41 that existed in 1939, 28 had been sunk by 1945.

But, despite setbacks to the fleets and the growing realisation that stocks were diminishing, World War II did not mean the end of whaling. A preliminary meeting of nations in London in 1944 looked at reintroducing the earlier convention's whaling restrictions in anticipation of future whaling efforts. As well as agreeing that Antarctic humpbacks should be further protected, it was at this meeting that the concept of restricting catches based on the questionable idea of a 'Blue Whale Unit' was introduced.

The basic idea of the Blue Whale Unit (BWU) was to try to equate whales by the amount of oil they yielded, so that they can be comparable. Thus, one blue whale produces approximately 20 tonnes of oil, which was as much oil as from 2 fin whales, or 2 ½ humpbacks, or 6 sei whales. So, a Blue Whale Unit was equivalent to: 1 blue whale, or 2 fins, or 2 ½ humpbacks, or 6 seis. It was a brave, but utterly misguided attempt to fix catch limits without making species distinctions.

Creating the IWC

Finally, in 1946 delegates from 19 countries attended the conference in Washington DC, which formed the International Whaling Commission (IWC), with the remit to **'provide for the proper conservation of whale stocks and thus make possible the orderly development of the whaling industry'.**[8] Although clearly focussed on ensuring a future for whaling, this was nonetheless a commendable aim. It was clear from the preface of the IWC's founding agreement that there was an understanding that whaling had been up 'until now, unsustainable. A quote from the Preface of the agreement creating the IWC shows that the effect of hunting on whale populations was well-known: **'Considering the history of whaling has seen the over-fishing of one area after another and of one species of whale after another to such a degree that it is essential to protect all species of whales from further over-fishing'.**[9] There were some pretty fundamental measures needed to attempt to protect all species of whales from (over) exploitation, namely: protecting immature animals; setting limits on animals captured; setting up sanctuaries or reserves free of hunting, and the complete prohibition of capture of endangered species. These are supposed to be the basic tenets of fisheries management the world over. Where whaling differed most importantly from fishing was in dealing with a much less-easily renewable resource.

But the IWC was beset with problems from the start. Reconciling the concerns of the whaling industry, politicians and scientists (a panel of whom were now incorporated into the IWC to monitor whale populations) was by no means easy. The problems were multiplied when the concerns of different nations were pitted against each other. In what would be a vain attempt, the IWC adopted an annual total quota of 16,000 Blue Whale Units for the Southern Ocean, a measure that was to prove entirely futile in protecting whale species from overfishing. This quota was arbitrarily set to be two thirds of the pre-war level of whales caught, on the assumption that the pre-war catches were understood to be excessive, but without knowing just how excessive they were. There were no limits by country or company, nor restrictions by species. Whaling would stop once the total 16,000 BWU quota for the year had been killed – effectively forcing all involved to do their best to catch as many big whales as they could, as quickly as they could. Because it was in each whaling fleet's interest to get as big a share as possible of this quota, the BWU limit led to a huge increase in the number of whale catching vessels, increasing whaling capacity instead of decreasing it. By the 1960s the average size of a factory whaling ship was 19,000 tonnes.

After the war, and despite complaints from Norway and Britain, the US allowed Japan to return to the whaling grounds, encouraging them to make use of whales for food. Whale meat was (and is) eaten in different ways, from choice cuts served raw as sashimi, to whale steaks, to canned meats and blubber used in soups. If whaling was to continue, there seemed to be no legitimate justification to exclude Japan. Whale meat from the Southern Ocean was to provide a crucial food source for Japan in the wake of the devastation of World War II. Japan only became a full member of the IWC in 1951.

The story of the IWC in the 20th Century has been described as: **'a sorry tale of commercial greed, blind self-interest, futile diplomacy, and callous disregard for the world's resources'.**[10]

But the biggest problem seemed to be that the maritime nations involved all held the freedom of the high seas as sacrosanct, indeed the tentative control of the whaling industry represented the first ever attempt to regulate activities on the high seas. That sadly meant they were either unwilling or unable to effectively control the remorseless overexploitation of the world's whale populations. Giving the IWC any real powers was a step too far. Like the blue whales whose destruction they were presiding over, the IWC was a great toothless beast.

Too much, too little, too late
It didn't take long to realise that the 16,000 BWU quota for the Antarctic was too high, but the reductions were not in line with any degree of urgency or caution... It was reduced very, very gradually so that by 12 years later, in 1958, the quota had only dropped to 14,500 BWU.

Not surprisingly the BWU didn't work, it was after all based on wishful thinking, rather than science, and crucially failed to incorporate any differentiation between whale species – allowing some to be grossly over-persecuted. The catch levels did decrease, but only because the amount of whales available to catch did: the damage had already been done. Whalers understandably targeted the blues first, then the fins, and so on down the species by sizes. The degree to which the species make-up in the Antarctic changed can be seen in the catch statistics.

Of the total amount of blue and fin whales caught, before 1933–34 80% were blues. Two decades later, in the 1953-54 season, the proportions had more than reversed, as more than 90% were fins, and less than 10% were blues.

Harpoonist at the prow of
a Japanese whaling vessel

Diminishing numbers of big whales meant that increasingly smaller whales were being targeted. In the 1953–54 season, 3 minke whales were listed in the pelagic whaling statistics – a species not targeted before because it wasn't worth the effort. To illustrate the minkes' lowly status to whalers, they didn't even feature in the BWU equation, as it would have taken so many to yield as much oil as a blue whale.

Other whales, notably the sperm whale, were still being hunted too, and whaling was not limited to the Southern Ocean but it was undoubtedly the site of the majority of the resources and catch. More efficient ships and advances in technology made whales previously out of reach or too-small-to-bother-with now worth hunting (a pattern that we can also see in industrialised fishing) began to be targeted.

In the North Atlantic the post-war years saw a resurgence in rorqual hunting to provide a precious food source in Norway, with minkes being the key targets. In the peak year of whaling (1949) 3,928 minkes, 34 orcas, and 221 northern bottlenose whales were killed.

By 1958, international whaling had to abide by yet more restrictions from the IWC: factory ships were only permitted to operate in the Antarctic and some regions of the North Pacific; whaling for rorquals elsewhere could only be carried out from land-based stations, and in tropical regions factory ships were restricted to targeting only sperm whales.

The 1959–60 season would mark the last full year of whaling by Britain, who had been a driving force in whaling for centuries. But sadly, the end of whaling for Britain and other countries came because their virtual extinction had made it a trade that was no longer profitable and cheaper alternatives for most whale products were becoming much more easily available anyway.

Blue whales gained full protection in
1965 – their numbers still have not recovered

Toothless regulation

In 1946, when the IWC was created, whales were considered a renewable resource like any other. From its very inception, the IWC was stymied by its own limitations – it couldn't restrict the numbers of vessels or shore stations, or change the system of quota allocations. Because any member nation who was not happy with any particular agreement could simply lodge an objection to it, the system was weak. Although the shortcomings of the IWC were clear, it was optimistically believed that it was better to have countries involved in some way than not at all. Better to be inside the tent, harpooning out, apparently.

Between 1958 and 1962 the IWC tried desperately to keep members onboard. Amidst walk-outs, threatened walk-outs, disagreements and dummy-spitting, the IWC was more concerned with protecting itself than the whales. So, in order not to antagonise any delicate members, they avoided any reductions in quotas. Because of the internal wrangling, each individual Antarctic whaling country was permitted to set their own quotas, the worst possible scenario, leading to an enormous catch of over 41,000 whales in 1960–61, the second largest catch in history.

After the rorqual numbers in the Southern Ocean had been drastically depleted, attention was focussed once again on the sperm whale, and the whaling industry largely moved to the North Pacific. In 1960, sperm whales accounted for a third of the world's catch of whales, and by 1967 there were more sperm whales killed than any other species. At its peak, almost 30,000 sperm whales were being killed every year.

Pirate whaling

On top of the over excesses of 'legitimate' whaling, there was also the issue of pirate whaling outwith the auspices of the IWC. The most notorious participant was Aristotle Onassis, working with ships registered in Panama, based in Uruguay, and with German crew. For four seasons from 1950–51 he thumbed his nose at regulations by the IWC and flaunted his illicit whaling operations by inviting business associates onboard to watch whales being killed, and adorning his private yacht with furniture upholstered with whale foreskin, and embellished with whale teeth. Pirate whaling was even more of a concern as there was not only no control over the amount of whales caught, there was also no regard for depleted or protected species, or immature animals. By the end of 1955, it was public intervention by the Norway government, coupled with a threat to seize his ship and its catch, which forced him to get out of the business. After profiting from four years of illegal whaling, Onassis sold his fleet to a Japanese company in 1956 – the vessels would be simply renamed and keep on killing whales.

In a way pirate whaling was a good thing for whale conservation, in pointing out just how futile the global regulation of the industry, was but the cost to already-troubled whales was high.

Lacklustre legacy

The IWC's legacy in protecting the world's whale populations is not a good one. During the first three decades of the IWC presiding over the regulation of whaling, and the protection of whale 'stocks', almost 1.5 million whales died. Despite getting formal protection by the IWC from its inception in 1946, Western gray whales, and North Atlantic rights continued to be hunted illicitly, and their numbers have still not recovered.

Things were starting to change, though. One by one, nations stopped their high seas whaling operations as scarcer supplies of whales, and cheaper man-made alternative products made the industry no longer worthwhile. The UK and New Zealand stopped in 1963, the Netherlands in 1964, and the Norway in 1968 (although they continued to hunt in their national waters).

By the end of the 1960s the remaining whaling nations were increasingly desperate for targets – blue whales were finally given full protection in 1965, by which time humpbacks were also fully protected – for those continuing to whale in the

Southern Ocean the focus shifted increasingly to smaller whales like sei, then minkes.

The failed BWU was eventually abandoned in 1972, to be replaced with a system of quotas based on the 'Maximum Sustainable Yield'. In theory that meant that quotas could be set at levels that would not affect stock levels. In banking terms, it's like just spending the interest on your money, but not spending the capital. In theory, that seems sensible, but it makes no allowances for lack of knowledge of stock levels, sub-populations social structures, and breeding patterns. And if that wasn't bad enough, there was an unseen problem – illegal whaling by IWC members and other nations that didn't figure on the catch statistics. As late as 1993 it was revealed that Soviet whaling fleets had ignored restrictions in whale quotas for decades, using falsified data to cover unreported catches of over 100,000 whales in the Southern Ocean alone. To make it even worse, many of these were (notionally) protected species.

But those still involved in whaling were to face another challenge in the latter decades of the 20th Century. The tide of public opinion on whaling was about to turn, led by the emerging environmental movement who were about to find a charismatic and enigmatic icon worth saving.

Greenpeace disrupts whaling by
obstructing a factory vessel

6 | Saving the whale

Reinventing the whale

My earliest memory of seeing real live cetaceans was when I was about 4 or 5 in Shetland, when there was a small group of harbour porpoises (**Phocoena phocoena**) in the harbour (conveniently enough!) in Scalloway. These are one of the smallest cetaceans, reaching a maximum of about two metres in length, and, for the most part being rather unobtrusive and shy.

At about the same time, elsewhere in the world the fate of the porpoises' bigger cousins was about to become big news, as Greenpeace, part of the fledgling environmental movement, started to campaign to Save The Whale. It became an iconic message that has stood the test of time – and a connection that virtually everyone will make when they hear the name Greenpeace, in no matter of time, is 'saving whales'. That makes me proud as a Greenpeace campaigner. And, seasickness notwithstanding, I feel privileged to have seen whales whilst at sea on all three of Greenpeace's current ships.

The most recent whale I've seen was also in Shetland waters, a brief glimpse of a minke whale as it surfaced in 'bumpy' seas next to the Greenpeace ship, the **Arctic Sunrise**. I was doing my best to hold on to both my lunch and the handrail as the ship rolled over 45 degrees in each direction, and was the only one on deck. No one else saw the whale as it fleetingly came up for breath in the wake of the ship, but it didn't matter, that brief glimpse made my day, and temporarily overcame my mal-de-mer.

By the early 1970s most of the nations who had been heavily involved in commercial whaling had stopped. There simply weren't enough whales left to make it worthwhile. Moreover a growing appreciation of wildlife, the environment in general, and of whales in particular, made whaling no longer easy to justify either. The upshot of the environmentalists championing the plight of the world's whale populations was to create a general awareness that we had gone too far, and pushed a group of amazing, enormous, advanced mammals to the brink of extinction. Growing public awareness was coupled with growing scientific awareness of the parlous state of some of the whale species and populations. Hunting had reduced humpbacks to a best-guess of 10%[11] of their former abundance, and blue whales to a mere 1%[12] of their guesstimated pre-whaling numbers: startling figures to be sure. What made the movement all the more real was that people were now willing to put themselves at risk to save the whales. Previously they may well have risked their lives to hunt whales, but this was very different.

Whales, tigers, pandas, and elephants became the ambassadors for a planet we seemed bent on trashing. The environmental movement was a wake-up call.

Greenpeace

Greenpeace cut its campaigning teeth protesting against nuclear testing, chartering a small fishing boat in 1971. The boat, which was renamed **Greenpeace** for the trip, set out from Vancouver with a crew of 12 to oppose the United States' testing of nuclear devices on an island off the coast of Alaska. Today Greenpeace is a campaigning organisation with a presence in over 40 countries worldwide, and some 2.8 million supporters.[13] Around the world Greenpeace campaigns on a range of environmental threats, from climate change to forests, oceans, energy and toxics. As an organisation known for its at-sea confrontations, Greenpeace is intrinsically linked to the oceans, and the anti-whaling images of Greenpeace are arguably its most iconic and enduring.

After the crash in whale populations, most countries had given up on high seas whaling, with two notable exceptions: Japan and the Soviet Union. As the big rorquals had been fished out and protection given to the endangered rights and grays, the focus was once again on the sperm whales, and also the smaller rorquals. Normal economics had made whaling impractical, but these countries were special cases – the Soviet whaling fleet was state-owned, so normal economic considerations did not apply. Japan, after being encouraged to make use of whales in the post-war period, was the only country with a ready market for whale meat, which had proved to be unpalatable to all of the other commercial whaling nations who had been exploiting the high seas. There were of course exceptions, such as Norway and Iceland, where coastal whaling in national waters was still occurring. Here too there was an appetite for whale meat, although it was generally limited to coastal communities with a traditional reliance on the meat.

Confronting Goliath

In 1975 Greenpeace started campaigning for whales – despite having limited resources and ability to engage the whalers, they were determined to confront and disrupt the Soviet and Japanese whaling operations in the North Pacific if they could. Even before they had left port their actions had already made whaling an international media issue, as the Japanese government, concerned about any protest directed at their fleet, publicly warned Greenpeace against interfering with their whaling, threatening legal action if they did. Greenpeace had made the decision to fully document their trip with cameras, which was to prove a wise move.

The first at-sea confrontation though was against the Soviet whaling fleet in 1975. Greenpeace set sail from Vancouver in Canada, to intercept the Soviet whaling fleet, and were seen off by a crowd of 23,000 well-wishers as they left port. Initially the contact with the whaling ship amounted to bearing witness and documenting the slaughter taking place. And it was a particularly bloody and gruesome scene, the sea around the whale processing vessel was red with whale blood. The whalers were bemused to find a boat load of protesters playing guitars and singing anti-whaling songs to them. They then played recordings of humpback whale song through loud-speakers. But it was not until the Greenpeace vessels headed after the harpoon boats, which had just set off to begin hunting that the sparks really began to fly. Moments later, Greenpeace had launched its small inflatable boats, and they were racing to position themselves between the harpoon guns and the whales. Ignoring the protest, and with apparently little concern for the protestors' safety the whalers fired a harpoon that flew directly over the Greenpeace inflatable, exploding in the back of a sperm whale right next to them.

The casual disregard for whale and human life was caught on camera – and the images quickly travelled around the world, being picked up in newswires throughout Europe, the US and even Japan. Although the whale in question died, the actions of Greenpeace on that day allowed several more to escape, and would set the foundation for a global campaign to stop whaling.

As the report in the **New York Times** said: '**For the first time in the history of whaling, human beings had put their lives on the line for whales**'.[14] Grass roots groups who wanted to get involved saving whales quickly sprang up throughout the US and Canada, and by 1976 Greenpeace had raised enough money to charter a faster ship to tackle the whalers. They could now keep up with the whaling fleet. The at-sea actions stepped up a gear, as the environmentalists again engaged the whaling fleet out at sea, some 2,250 kilometres southwest of San Francisco. This time one of the inflatable boats, in an attempt to stop a sperm whale carcass being taken onboard the factory ship (to hinder their operations), ended up being hauled out of the water along with the whale. They harassed and confounded the Soviet whalers for a total of 10 days. Although they did not find the Japanese whaling fleet, it later emerged that, given the high levels of anti-whaling sentiment amongst the public, Japanese vessels had been 'advised' to make sure they were not in the area. In disrupting the hunt and displacing the whalers, Greenpeace claimed that their successful second whale-saving trip had directly saved about 100 individual whales, and by forcing the Japanese fleet out of its whaling grounds may have indirectly saved over 1,000 more.

Warriors of the Rainbow

But the fight against commercial whaling would not just be won on the high seas. In 1977 Greenpeace's flagship, the **Rainbow Warrior** (a converted Scottish trawler) set sail for the first time from London, destined for Iceland, and the Icelandic whaling fleet. The iconic vessel's maiden voyage went via Britain's east coast, passing many ex-whaling ports, and even refueled in Shetland, where Salvesen's whaling business had fledged less than a century before.

Most nations had by now stopped whaling, but a few persisted. Greenpeace's strategy was to target the whalers around the world, as well as the most obvious 'villains' (the large Soviet and Japanese fleets), the other nations still whaling were keeping an unacceptable industry alive. Ultimately the environmentalists wanted to force the IWC into adopting stronger conservation measures, including a ban on commercial whaling, which had been called for internationally at the United Nations environment conference five years earlier.

At the time Iceland was the only country still killing fin whales, despite stocks being internationally recognised as depleted. The four austere harpoon-wielding catcher boats which sit proudly in Reykjavik harbour to this day were, together with a Norwegian fleet, intent on catching 2,500 whales in the North Atlantic over the summer of 1977.

Icelandic whaling

Iceland is a beautiful country, with a deeply-indented coastline creating countless sheltered fjords. One such fjord is Hvalfjördur (which literally translates as 'whale fjord'). Famously this region of Iceland is rich in cetacean diversity, but the sinister side to the place is that it is also the site of a shore whale processing station. I visited the bleak place in 2003, on a rather dismal day in early autumn. It was apparently abandoned, and it looked like it had been left in a hurry. Although the equipment was in relatively good condition (indeed it would be put back to use only a few years later as part of a small, but hugely controversial fin whale

hunt) the place looked like it had shut down very quickly. There were stacks of flat-packed cardboard boxes printed in Japanese writing for exporting meat, and coats and boots hung up on lockers as if the place had been deserted just days before.

The huge slipway leading down to the water was eerily empty, as John Burton, a British ex-whaler objectively talked us through how the grisly process of landing and processing a large whale would have happened. Behind the station whale bones lay mouldering in the overgrown grass.

Some 25 years earlier, it was from this fjord that Iceland's whaling fleet was due to emerge, and the **Rainbow Warrior** sat at its mouth awaiting them. But Greenpeace were to be outrun by the whalers who were faster and better able to handle the unruly weather off Iceland. After 10 days they finally managed to disrupt the hunt, getting between fin whales and Icelandic harpoons. The whalers gave up and returned to port. The **Rainbow Warrior** would continue to disrupt the hunt for a further month. By the time Greenpeace left Iceland, as well as saving many whales, they had made whaling a major issue for Iceland too. The **Rainbow Warrior's** first campaigning trip had been a resounding success.

Image on facing page:
A fin whale is dragged up the slipway of
the whaling station at Hvalfjördur in Iceland

Persisting pirates

Restrictions imposed by the IWC gave full protection to some species, like grays, rights and blues, and annual quotas were allocated to IWC member nations for species that were still allowed to be killed. But it wasn't just this legitimate (albeit indefensible) whaling that was the issue, pirate whaling was still happening too, which was even more of an environmental scandal as it was indiscriminate and unregulated. The **Rainbow Warrior** would go on to be arrested for five months in Spain in 1980, after Spanish authorities took exception to Greenpeace disrupting Spanish whaling vessels engaged in pirate whaling near the port of Vigo.

The same year the IWC met in Brighton, in England. They were certainly made aware of the illicit Spanish whaling, and Greenpeace lobbyists were making headway from within the IWC meeting as well as in front of whaling vessels. The meeting cut quotas further (albeit not enough) and for the first time brought orcas (not a 'Great whale') under the quota system. There was also a vote on a 10 year moratorium, or ban, on commercial whaling, which only narrowly failed.

Pirate whaling was still an issue, but despite Onassis' operations being brought to the IWC's attention as far back as 1955 it would not be until 1979 that it became a headline issue. Undercover work by Greenpeace and other conservation groups revealed that some IWC members (in particular Norway and Japan) were buying whale products from non-IWC countries. Many countries, such as Brazil, Chile, South Korea, and Spain were whaling outwith the IWC's auspices, but with financial support, equipment, and expertise being provided from Japan.

Perhaps the most controversial pirate vessel of the time was the **Sierra**, which was owned by Norwegians, sailing under

Image on preceding page:
Greenpeace inflatable between catcher
and factory whaling vessels

a Somalian flag, registered in Leichtenstein, operated by South Africans, and crewed with Japanese technicians. The **Sierra** was illicitly selling meat to Japan, and oil to Norway and the EEC. The **Sierra** was killing whatever whales it could find, including endangered species like blues and rights, and juvenile whales too. However, it was not any effective regulation or policing that stopped the **Sierra**, or indeed two other Spanish vessels involved in illegal whaling, but extremist saboteurs who sunk all three vessels in port.

Greenpeace meanwhile published undercover evidence of illegal Taiwanese whaling that was supplying meat to Japan, exposing the scandal immediately before the IWC meeting in 1980. The ensuing embarrassment led Japan to ban further shipments from Japan, and led to the decommissioning of the Taiwanese whaling vessels in 1981.

The end of whaling?

Commercial whaling, legal and illegal, was being opposed around the world. It was being obstructed at sea, and confronted in the lobbies of government, and the murky dealings of an unpleasant industry were being exposed to the world. Whaling was becoming an increasingly difficult industry to justify.

Inside the IWC, as in the outside world, the balance of power was shifting too, in favour of the whales. New 'pro-conservation' members were swelling the IWC's ranks at the behest of other governments and in the light of the global public concern about the world's whales fired-up by the environmentalists. Most of the members no longer had a whaling industry, and the revelations of pirate whaling made it more likely for governments to want to come down in favour of stronger regulation to protect remaining whale populations. Hunting sperm whales was banned in 1981, but the commission again failed to agree a moratorium on commercial whaling. Just one year later, in 1982, the international hourglass seemed to have run out for commercial whaling. At the IWC meeting members voted by 25 to 7 (with 5 abstentions) to end all commercial whaling in three years time, and impose a moratorium on commercial whaling. It was an historic achievement not only for the environmentalists and conservationists, but also for the IWC, which was, after all, set up by whalers to ensure a future for whalers.

Enforcing the ban

As with many environmental victories however, the newly agreed ban was about to be undermined. Within five months, four of the remaining eight countries involved in commercial whaling had filed objections to the ban. The objecting nations were the Soviet Union, Japan, Norway and Peru. Perhaps understandably, Greenpeace was determined to make them change their mind, and the **Rainbow Warrior** headed to Peru. There, activists, buoyed by support from the Peruvian fishing industry for a ban on whaling, chained themselves to a whaling vessel, and the Greenpeace ship was again arrested, but freed a few weeks later.

Six months later, timed to coincide with the 1983 IWC meeting, Greenpeace headed to Soviet waters to confront their fleet. The whaling they were drawing attention to was targeting the threatened stock of Western grays, and seemed to be using the loophole of aboriginal whaling to provide cheap meat for feeding captive animals like mink and foxes in fur farms: an outrageous waste of an endangered species, for an industry that was also becoming increasingly unpalatable. The **Rainbow Warrior** was chased across the Bering Sea by a Soviet gunboat, and several activists were arrested. The mission made front page news across the world, and public support forced the Soviet authorities into releasing the Greenpeace activists. In an attempt to forcibly keep a lid on their whaling operation, the Soviets had given it worldwide coverage.

Pressure was kept up on the remaining whaling nations, particularly Japan and the Soviet Union. Protests and demonstrations worldwide targeted their embassies, and direct actions were undertaken by Greenpeace to oppose the whaling operations by both countries in the Southern Ocean, as well as

Icelandic graffiti shows growing
domestic criticism of the country's
whaling programme

the Norwegian whaling fleet.

The moratorium on commercial whaling came into effect
in 1986, but before that had happened, some were already
doing their best to get around it. In 1985 the Japanese Fisheries
Minister, Moriyoshi Sato, claimed that his government would:
**'do its utmost to find ways to maintain the nation's whaling in
the form of research or other forms'.**[15]

There was also a growing understanding of the increasing
impact humans were having on whale populations and the rest
of the world as the world got to know more about pollution, over
consumption, and the global environment. The IWC's ban on
commercial whaling was however not to be the end of the story.
Whaling continued, both blatantly and via convenient loopholes.

7

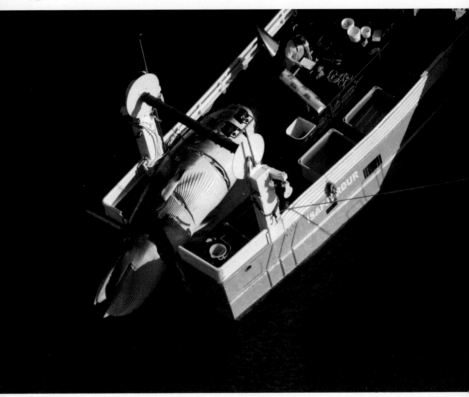

Minke whales are hunted close to shore
by small boats in Iceland, as in Norway

7 | Where we are today

Failing on whaling

The agreement to a ban on commercial whaling was of course a major victory for conservation, an inspirationally visionary move, and great news for whales. In a matter of decades, countries like the UK, Australia, and the US had gone from being whale-killers to whale-savers. The public loved whales, viewing them as some mammalian ambassadors for all life on earth and taking comfort in the fact that if we can save these, the biggest animals on our planet, then there must, surely, be hope for us smaller animals too.

A large amount of the focus on the whaling issue was not just on the state of the populations, and the very real threat of driving species and populations to the brink of extinction, but also that it was a particularly gruesome, barbaric and painful activity. Once you know whales are large mammals, with big brains and complex communication and social groups, the jump to caring about their welfare is not great. And the images of whaling were anything but clean, efficient, or humane.

I don't want to dwell too much on the welfare issue – to me it's a bit of a no-brainer. If you care about animal welfare, whaling is not a good thing. But even if that is not a concern, or a major concern for you, it's clear that there's a very real difference between raising and slaughtering an animal for meat, and pursuing and killing one at sea. It's also obvious that dispatching a fast-moving animal weighing tens of tonnes, and many metres long is not likely to be a humane or quick activity. In short, there is no humane way to kill a whale at sea. But even if that doesn't prick your conscience, the simple fact is that commercial whaling was an exceptionally unsustainable industry, and I doubt many considerate or thinking people really think that relentless persecution to extinction is a good thing.

Nevertheless, many groups took up the cause for whales, including consideration of the welfare of the individual animals.

The moratorium was eventually agreed in 1982, to come into force in 1986. However, as we have already seen, the IWC is not a particularly efficient organisation at enforcing its decisions – so 1986 would not see the end of commercial whaling.

Who's still whaling?

So, what's the situation today, more than 20 years after the commercial whaling ban came into place... and why on earth is whaling even still an issue?

Iceland

Whaling in Iceland is in a precarious place at the moment. They previously left the IWC ostensibly in protest at the whaling ban, and conducted 'scientific' whaling too. Recently the scientific whaling was restarted after a gap of some 14 years. Initially this was at very small numbers and on relatively-uncontentious species (they announced an intention to target a few hundred in total, of three species, but changed this to smaller numbers, and only minke whales) and they were keen to be seen to be 'reasonable' in the face of international condemnation and outrage from environmentalists, conservationists, and members of the public. In 2006 they added a commercial whaling quota – for fin and minke. The market for meat is very small and diminishing, there is simply not enough local demand to justify any degree of whaling, particularly when it is such a contentious issue. The situation at present is uncertain, but for the first time there is a significant part of the Icelandic population questioning, and opposing, whaling – which they see as entirely unnecessary, and bad for both their image and economy.

Iceland's previous 'scientific' whaling programme was heavily opposed by conservation and environmental groups. Indeed, boycotts of Iceland and Icelandic goods were used, resulting in the suspension of the whaling programme in 1989. They have also left and recently rejoined the IWC: rather bizarrely and contentiously they rejoined in 2002 but did so with an objection to the commercial whaling moratorium. Effectively they joined up with the equivalent of a prenuptial agreement, despite the fact that no other nation has enjoyed this privilege. This is all the more puzzling, as, before they left the IWC in 1991, they had actually agreed to the moratorium. As mentioned before, the idea that it's better to have half-hearted participation rather than none still seems to pervade the IWC.

Norway

Norway is in the IWC but had lodged an objection to the moratorium in 1992, thereafter they returned to whaling. Norwegian commercial whaling operations are undertaken outwith any IWC control, and with no need to use the loophole of 'science'. Their whaling operation targets minke whales, using relatively small boats, and essentially just in coastal waters. In keeping with Japan's provocative increases in self-appointed quotas, Norway too has upped its own quotas over recent years. This is a deliberately provocative move, and was accompanied by the suggestion that they would not confine themselves to their own waters.

Throughout the 1990s the numbers hunted were between 200 and 600 whales, but in 2005 the unilateral quota was increased to almost 800 whales, and this was raised further to 1,052 in 2007. In reality, the Norwegian quota is rarely met in full, there is neither the capacity to hunt the whales, nor enough market for the meat. By inflating the quota, Norway adds weight to the perception that there are plenty of whales to hunt, and also makes sure it does not fall foul of sex discrimination if they end up taking too many female whales (the quota is supposed to be a 50:50 sex ratio). Female minkes are of course, bigger than males, and whalers are still trigger happy for the biggest whales they can get.

The blubber from Norwegian minkes is no longer landed, it is discarded at sea, being dangerously toxic. So even with only the choicest meat being taken to port, Norway is still struggling for domestic demand to live up to the whaling hype. Warnings over toxins in the whale meat from the polluted waters of the

North Sea and North Atlantic probably don't help sales either.

Japan

Initially Japan did not agree to end its commercial whaling operation, but then relented and said it would give up by 1988, and they do technically recognise the moratorium.

However, they immediately announced plans to return to the Antarctic to conduct 'research' whaling. Initially this was for just a couple of years, killing roughly 270 whales each year, but was extended and repeated. Japan has been using the loophole of 'scientific' whaling ever since – and the numbers and species being caught has been increased over the years. Bearing in mind that for 'scientific' whaling there is no allocated quota by the IWC or any international body; the quota is entirely and arbitrarily decided by the country carrying out the whaling.

In 1994 (the same year ironically that the IWC created the Southern Ocean Whale Sanctuary – which Japan does not recognise) Japan expanded the scope of its 'scientific' whaling programme, by starting to whale in the North Pacific too. The North Pacific whaling programme currently hunts roughly 220 minkes, 100 seis, 50 Bryde's, and 10 sperm whales each year.

In 2005 the self-allocated quota for the Southern Ocean was more than doubled to 850 minke whales. Ten percent more or less is permitted, and unsurprisingly the Japanese fleet usually try to catch exactly '+10%'. As well as the increase in minkes, 10 fin whales (which are still endangered) were added to the list, and it was announced then that by the 2007–08 season they would be taking 50 fin, and 50 humpback whales.

Japan's total self-allocated quota is about 1,400 Great whales each year. Allegedly these whales die for science, whilst recognising a global ban on commercial whaling.

As everyone knows, the meat from this ends up on sale – and the Government of Japan claim that this is necessary and required, when it is clearly just a way of being able to whale commercially 'legitimately' and appear to respect international opinion. If any evidence were needed that this is about commerce in the long term as well as the short term – then the scientific programme itself gives the game away as it is specifically designed to ascertain if the populations of whales can be sustainably hunted, and at what level. So, in effect the science that gets round the ban on commercial whaling is designed to justify and enable a return to commercial whaling!

Japan is the principal nation actively working within the IWC to attempt to overturn the moratorium and restart commercial whaling. In doing this they seem to be seeking the legitimacy of the IWC although they publicly threaten to leave the organisation on an almost annual basis. The evidence that suggests they would rather have legitimacy from within is vast. The Fisheries Agency of Japan has spent millions of yen supporting their ailing whaling industry, marketing whale products, lobbying at the IWC, and even in buying votes at the IWC through fisheries aid to developing countries. Japan has found itself a complicated and controversial way to continue to hunt whales (mostly on the high seas) for the commercial market within the auspices and rules of the IWC, and in theory they respect the moratorium! This is in direct contrast to Norway, whose objection to the ban is what enables them to hunt unhindered (almost exclusively in national waters). The Government of Japan continues to claim that the moratorium is only 'temporary' and repeatedly urges the international community to return to 'normality', by which they mean resume commercial whaling for anyone who wants to.

As well financially supporting their whaling industry, the Government of Japan is also funding an internal campaign to market whale meat. Faced with large stockpiles of unsold meat this has been given to schools, made into burgers in a vain attempt to market it to young consumers, and even been discovered in pet food. The official figures reveal that some 3,161 tonnes of whale meat was stockpiled in Japan in February 2007, and 2,485 tonnes in February 2008.[16]

It's worth remembering that these stockpiles would be greater still if it weren't for direct action by Greenpeace and

others disrupting the hunts, and the fire aboard the factory ship in 2007 that drew a premature end to the whaling season. In the most recent Southern Ocean whaling season, disruption by environmental activists meant that only 551 of their quota of 935 minke whales were caught by the Japanese fleet. As the whalers try to use this information to attack those that oppose their hunt, we should also take note that the 2007–08 Southern Ocean whaling expedition failed to kill any of its self-allocated quota of 50 fin whales. Why? Well, because they couldn't find any… suggesting that perhaps the species is considered 'endangered' for good reason!

As if that toll of great whales being killed wasn't enough, there are other cetaceans still being hunted too. As well as the quotas allocated by the IWC for Aboriginal Subsistence Whaling, there are commercial hunts for small cetaceans that are entirely unregulated by the IWC. The notable perpetrators are the Faroes, who kill several hundred pilot whales in 'the Grind' every year, and Japan, who prosecute drive hunts for an assortment of small cetaceans (dolphins, pilot whales etc.) and one very large hunt for a specific small cetacean – the Dall's porpoise **(Phocoenoides dalli)**.

This porpoise is a striking black and white animal, found in the waters of the North Pacific. At about 2 metres long, it's quite big for a porpoise, but not big for a cetacean. But what the porpoises lack in stature, the Japanese make up for in volume – killing 17–20,000 of these animals annually, without even having to report the methods of hunting used to the IWC. In 1988 it peaked at a staggering 40,000 animals. This is a largely overlooked cetacean hunt that largely ends up ascanned 'whale' meat in Japanese supermarkets (and is often mislabelled as 'minke').

Image on facing page:
A minke whale that eventually drowns,
thrashes and wrenches its own flesh apart
trying to escape the harpoons

Canned 'whale meat' on sale in Japan
is regularly mislabelled, and can contain
dolphin and porpoise meat

The IWC today

The IWC today is still a toothless giant, with a very polarised membership that doesn't really reflect the world, or indeed global views on whales. Moreover, successful attempts to politicise the organisation mean that many who are members have little or no direct concern with the plight of whales either. Recently the membership has been rising due to the Government of Japan's aggressive vote-buying campaign, tying Overseas Development Aid (ODA) particularly to Pacific, Caribbean and African countries, in return for their joining the IWC and voting with Japan.

Because of the way the IWC works, the numbers and indeed positions of member states are uncertain until the meeting. Effectively the IWC is an annual meeting where member nations get together to make agreements and resolutions, which they are then supposed to implement individually. Effectively therefore, the IWC does not exist outwith its annual meetings. In the intervening months new recruits to the IWC may be announced, but frequently unannounced new members turn up at the meeting, and some existing members fail to show. It may well add to the excitement, but it certainly doesn't make for a better functioning international body!

Buying legitimacy

It's now a matter of public record that Japan uses its diplomatic power and Fisheries ODA budget to recruit supporters within the IWC. In 2005 the Solomon Islands admitted that their attendance had been effectively paid for by the Government of Japan for the previous decade. It has similarly been shown that the Japanese had paid for Dominica, and Grenada too. Recent converts to Japan's side in the IWC are often suspiciously vociferous proponents of the pervasive 'whales-eat-fish' line, which perniciously casts whales as fish-munching villains, snatching the food out of the mouths of developing nations. For pro-whalers that helpfully sidesteps any complicated issues like factoring in the precautionary principle, as well as sidestepping any basis in fact. After all, if you say something often enough, people will start to believe it.

Since 2000 some 17 countries have been recruited to the IWC by Japan: Benin, Cambodia, Cote D'Ivoire, Gabon, Gambia, Guinea-Bissau, Guinea, Kiribati, Lao, Mali, Marshall Islands, Mauritania, Morocco, Nauru, Palau, Suriname and Tuvalu. The Government of Japan call this 'vote recruitment', opponents of whaling see it clearly as vote-buying, in an attempt to buy majority support within the IWC to overturn the commercial whaling ban.

Even if it were true that the countries involved would be concerned enough to join the IWC, we must surely question their priorities. Many of the same countries have not joined other international forums because the membership was prohibitively expensive. It is also hard to see how land-locked Mali could have whaling high on its political list of priorities.

At the 2006 IWC meeting the pro-whalers' block snatched a narrow majority of one and was able to cite IWC support for the so-called 'St. Kitts Declaration' which, amongst other things, stated as fact that, **'whales consume huge quantities of fish, making the issue a matter of food security'**, and declaring the moratorium **'no longer necessary'**.[17]

The majority was temporary but numbers on the IWC are still finely balanced, with only about 75 members at present, and perpetual pressure on both sides to have new recruits at each ensuing meeting. This constant battle for numbers means that the organisation remains stymied from doing effective work (particularly in the realm of conservation) by blocks of members sceptical at the motives of other blocks. It also makes onlookers, particularly the global media, increasingly disinterested in all of this, and disillusioned with the IWC and the issues around whaling. There are a number of losers in this: the sanctity of international agreements; the taxpayers of Japan; the nominally pro-whaling countries recruited, whose people often know little about what is being said in their name, and the whales.

Opposing conservation

In 2004 the IWC agreed to set up a Conservation Committee to look at the many threats facing the world's remaining whale populations. Although that committee does exist it has been frustrated from doing any real work, by the same nations working within the IWC, to overturn the moratorium on commercial whaling. Presumably this stems from a concern that any pro-conservation focus from the IWC is a move against whaling. On top of that there is a perennial disagreement over the competency of the IWC.

NGOs and conservation minded countries insist that 'all whales' means 'all cetaceans', whereas pro-whaling countries insist that it only means 'Great whales'. The reason for this is complicated, and relates to the initial list of commercially-important whale species drawn up by the nascent IWC in the 1940s. Ironically, a shift in focus to smaller species would actually draw attention to abject failings by many of the most pro-conservation countries too – but primarily it would require involvement in the at-present unregulated hunting of small cetaceans that takes place in several countries.

The reality is that whilst the IWC remains polarised and paralysed, spending most of its time and effort on the debate over the continued hunting of species like minkes, other whales are also hunted, entirely free of any attempt at regulation. Bizarrely, Baird's beaked whales (**Berardius bairdii**), which can grow to be almost 13 metres long, are classified as 'small cetaceans', despite being bigger than minkes, which are considered 'Great whales'. This unfortunate anomaly of IWC history means that Baird's beaked whales can be (and are) hunted by Japan with no regulation, and total impunity.

To use a clichéd analogy, the IWC is currently a game of chess, which seems to be in a permanent stalemate.

8

Japanese whalers conducting 'science'
in the Southern Ocean Whale Sanctuary

8 | Weird Science

Getting around the moratorium

'Scientific whaling' is an odd concept. It's basically whaling, with the added nuisance of dressing it up as some sort of research. Doing some counting, weighing, taking some samples, allows you to then cut up the choicest meat, freeze it, and send it home to be sold for profit. It is estimated that some four-fifths of the cost of the current Japanese whaling operation in the Southern Ocean is funded by selling the whalemeat, with the remainder of the costs being met by the Government of Japan. Can you imagine the uproar if other scientific test subjects were on sale in your local supermarket? It is, in short, commercial whaling with a bit of window dressing.

I apologise in advance for the amount of inverted commas used when talking about 'scientific whaling', but to be honest I just can't bring myself to justify large-scale commercial whaling programmes.

The reason behind dressing it up as 'science', which sounds just as authoritative applied to whaling as it does when they use it as an advertising rationale for you to buy some new overpriced shampoo or cosmetics, is simple: if it's 'scientific' then the whaling is not considered commercial, and so is not technically prohibited by the moratorium. To make it even more attractive as an option, countries get to set their own quotas for whaling in the name of science, and their science programme doesn't need to be endorsed, requested or supported by anyone else. In fact 'scientific whaling' in general, and the Japanese whaling in the Southern Ocean in particular, have received repeated criticism, condemnation, and calls to cease by the IWC. There have also been frequent diplomatic appeals from many governments to cease scientific whaling, but they have carried on regardless. As loopholes go, whaling for 'science' is a great one, and conveniently big enough to sail a whaling fleet and several thousand whales through.

The extent of the experiment

At present, the Japanese whaling fleet conducts 'scientific' whaling in the Pacific (where they target sei, minke and sperm whales) and the Antarctic. The latter is most contentious because the area they hunt whales in is globally recognised as the Southern Ocean Whale Sanctuary. In 2007–08 the self-appointed quota in the Southern Ocean was 850 minke whales, 50 fin whales, and 50 humpback whales. Given that the announced quota can be exceeded by up to 10%, a total of 935 minkes could be killed 'acceptably', despite not having any endorsement outside of the Japanese government.

Fin whales are still classified as endangered, and humpbacks are classed as threatened (the humpbacks got a last-minute reprieve in the 2007–08 season, as a result of widespread outrage at the world's most photogenic whales being killed, but they are still in the sights of the whalers for future hunting. It remains to be seen whether adding humpbacks to the target list was just an elaborate political bluff to divert attention from the other whales being killed). Over the past few years Japan has provocatively increased its self-allocated quota, in 2005 they nearly doubled the amount of minke whales they intended to hunt, from 440 to 850.

Adding new species to the list is also a very provocative move, both in trying to assert that these species are now plentiful enough to be hunted, and in offering a bartering tool to appear more reasonable if they backed down over the more threatened and contentious species, whilst getting away with ramping up the scale of the minke whale hunt, thereby perpetuating a general acceptance of at least some of the whaling operation.

In the wider global context, the other countries involved in whaling are simultaneously trying to gain acceptance for whaling, by increasing quotas in Norway (irrespective of demand for meat or ability to catch them) and restarting 'scientific' and then commercial whaling in Iceland. Blatantly coincidentally Japan's announcement that they were to add fin whales to their hunt was followed by an announcement by Iceland that they too were to restart killing fin whales commercially, whilst at the same time spearheading moves to try and get the species' conservation status downgraded, and pave the way for exporting whale meat to Japan.

The irony is that in Japan, Norway and Iceland, whaling is a marginal concern, and directly affects very few people. The demand for whale meat in these countries is steadily diminishing, so any attempt to re-start an international trade in whale products would be doing so without any market. Indeed, Japan doesn't even want whale meat from the North Atlantic anyway, as it's considered too toxic!

Counting whales

'Lethal research' is accompanied by data from 'spotter' vessels that sail as part of the whaling fleet to the Antarctic. Their job is to collect sightings data of whales that in theory can be used to extrapolate estimates of populations in a given area. I've done some cetacean-spotting in the English Channel aboard the Greenpeace ship, the **Esperanza**. For us it was a (usually) bitterly cold and often seemingly unrewarding exercise, scanning the horizon for a breaking fin, or splash, but the point was to establish, by adhering to a scientific sampling protocol, what species of whales, dolphins and porpoises were in the area, and if possible try and use the data gathered to estimate the likely populations of the animals we had seen in the area.

That is not an easy thing to do – if there's one thing that we know about cetaceans, it's that there's a heck of a lot we don't know, and there are a huge amount of variables and caveats needed in any counting operation. Some animals are shy of vessels and some are inquisitive. Some are easier to spot than others. Most are almost impossible to see if the weather and visibility conditions are poor. And we know very little from spotting data other than a 'snapshot' of given species in a given area, at a given time. The truth is, there just isn't enough observation or understanding of cetacean populations in most areas of the world. This becomes even more problematic in an area like the Southern Ocean. In the Antarctic summer whales are generally there to feed. That means they will be where the prey is (or perhaps where they think it should be). Remember whales, like almost every other animal and plant on earth, are not evenly distributed. So any information we can get from sightings data, whilst valuable, is always going to be limited in what it can tell us. It says nothing of population structures or migration routes for example. There are often high margins of error with such population data, because of the unknown variables, and that causes enormous problems for anyone who is trying to use that data to set any sort of catch limits. For example – the minke whale population in the southern hemisphere, despite being one of the most intensively 'sampled' and well-surveyed, has shown an apparent decrease of 60% in 15 years, casting huge doubts over the strength of population estimates.[18]

Cynics (and I am often to be found masquerading as one) would raise a disbelieving eyebrow at the presence of spotter vessels as part of the whaling fleet anyway. Just how independent are they? True there are no harpoons on board, but one can speculate that having an extra couple of ships relaying the positions of abundant whales would be a boon to anyone looking to kill a thousand or so...

The cost of ear wax

So – what is this 'scientific' whaling supposed to tell us? In a recent BBC radio interview, the Japanese government representative's response as to why they must kill whales to conduct scientific study on them was, quite simply '**ear wax**'.[19] However, we should wipe all comical images of giant cotton buds from our minds, as the rationale of collecting these 'ear wax' samples means that in killing whales, 'scientific' whalers often aim the harpoon away from the brains, so as not to damage the samples. The result tends to be even more suffering for the whales.

The Fisheries Agency of Japan says it's vital to kill whales to better understand how long they live, and what they eat. One of the ways they estimate age is by studying the wood-like wax plugs from whales (internal) ears. The dead whales are also measured, have tissue samples taken, and their stomach contents recorded. It's a bit like cutting down a tree to work out how old it is. Or dissecting a panda just to make sure it had been eating bamboo and hadn't been sneakily eating burgers behind your back.

It would surely cause an outcry if this was happening to pandas, or tigers, even in the name of 'science', and rightly so.

Just to flit briefly back to the welfare issue, the majority of the female whales killed in Japan's scientific whaling in the Antarctic waters are pregnant. As far back as the Convention for the Regulation of Whaling in 1931, it was agreed to prohibit the hunting of immature whales as a clearly unsustainable activity, yet in the 2006–07 season, more than half of the minke whales killed were gestating: 92% of the female whales 'sampled' to death, were pregnant.[20] The high rates of pregnancy in slaughtered whales was actually spun as 'good news' by Japan's Institute of Cetacean Research, apparently showing that populations were healthy, fertile, and presumably could be whaled a bit more.

What the science tells us...

The outcome of this science has been at best shoddy, and at worst laughable – in the initial scientific programme, some 6,778 whales were killed in the Southern Ocean Whale Sanctuary over the space of 18 years. One of the stated aims was to work out the longevity of the southern hemisphere minke whales. The results? The margin of error was so broad that they didn't even rule out the possibility that minke whales were immortal (assuming they don't encounter any harpoons). The possibility that minke whales might be so resilient perhaps explains why the former Japanese Fisheries Minister Masayuki Komatsu famously referred to them as the 'cockroaches' of the sea.[21] If only whales were as resilient as cockroaches...

And what does the 'science' tell us about what whales are eating? Well, it's not earth-shattering, but apparently the

Image on preceding page:
The scant remains of the carcass of a
whale apparently killed for its ear plugs

Image above:
Cartons of frozen 'scientific research',
en route to the supermarkets or the
whale meat stockpile

minke whales in the Southern Ocean are predominantly eating krill, and in the northern hemisphere, where krill are less abundant than in the Antarctic, the proportions of small fish eaten are a bit higher.

None of this science needs to happen by hunting whales. And if a scientific research programme was needed that involved lethal research of a population of whales in international waters, then it should presumably be at the behest of, and with the authority of, an international body concerned with the state of the world's whale populations, like, say the IWC. Presumably too, it should not happen in an internationally-recognised whale sanctuary! Yet despite frequent protestations by the Japanese government that this research was asked for by the IWC, it was not. This is simply a way of continuing commercial whaling with a veneer of international credibility until such times as the moratorium is overturned and they can again whale commercially honestly. This conveniently also keeps the whaling fleet in commission, the whalers in jobs, and maintains a supply of whale meat to the marketplace – all of which, if allowed to lapse or fall into disrepair, would be major obstacles to resuming commercial whaling at a later date.

Seriously, can you imagine walking into your local supermarket to find tiger or gorilla steaks in the freezer? Or can you imagine the success of some laboratory trying to sell the meat from some animal testing research? Nowhere else do the products of scientific research end up in freezers, food cans (where they are often badly or incorrectly labelled) and sushi restaurants.

The real motivation?
The whaling debate often gets fiercely and unpleasantly nationalistic. In much the same way as European nations often blame another country for being solely responsible for taking 'their' fish, unfairly the entire nation of Japan is often tarnished as inconsiderate whale-eaters: a misapprehension that couldn't be further from the truth. A poll for the **Asahi** newspaper of

3,000 people in Japan in 2002 showed that only a very small minority of people, some 4%, eat whale meat regularly, with 86% of respondents either having never eaten it, or not eaten it since childhood. For most people in Japan whaling is not even an issue, and only a very small minority eat whale meat with any degree of regularity.

This tends to be in areas where coastal whaling has been a traditional source of food for centuries, and also tends to be more common amongst older generations, who remember eating whale meat in their youth. Of course, travelling thousands of miles to the Southern Ocean is not 'traditional whaling', and irrespective of whether it can ever be sustainable in terms of numbers, it certainly is not a sustainable activity from an environmental perspective.

The argument often used is that opponents of whaling do not understand or respect Japan's whaling traditions, and are trying to foist Western ideals upon them, despite the fact that many of the most pro-conservation countries themselves had international whaling industries, which they have duly abandoned. And lest we forget, large-scale, long-distance whaling in Japan was a 20th Century development.

What tissue samples and sampling of whale meat on sale has shown us repeatedly is that whales from the Southern Ocean have much lower levels of toxins in their flesh. That's good news for anyone thinking about eating them. There's a general pattern that the baleen whales that feed lower down the food chain on small fish and plankton have lower burdens of persistent pollutants. Animals that feed further up the food chain, such as the toothed whales, big predatory fish like tuna and swordfish, and polar bears, have much higher levels of contaminants. In whales, the particularly nasty stuff is often even more concentrated in the blubber, which is one of the reasons that the blubber is usually discarded at sea these days rather than landed to be sold. Repeated warnings have been issued about the levels of contaminants, including recommendations that pregnant women and nursing mothers should avoid eating whale meat. It's also the case that northern waters, like the North Pacific and North Atlantic, near the industrialised nations have more pollutants than the Antarctic. Indeed one of the reasons the Antarctic and Southern Ocean is so special and worthy of protection is for its relatively pristine state.

Clearly any claim on the Southern Ocean whales as a traditional food source (by any nation) is entirely bogus. But, as the only nation who really prosecuted the Antarctic waters for whale meat for human consumption, it is clear why the less-polluted whales from the far south present a more attractive option than more locally available whales. Ironically, a poll of the Japanese public (whose taxes subsidise the whaling programme) in February 2008 showed that 69%[22] did not support their Government's whaling programme in the Southern Ocean.

Of course, another reason why dependence on local-to-Japan whales is problematic is that the waters there no longer have many whales. Centuries of shore-based hunting have taken their toll, and as with waters around most of the developed world, other human activities are also impacting badly on whales. There is also an insidious back-door supply of whale meat in Japan and neighbouring South Korea. Around the world whales, dolphins and porpoises are caught and killed in fishing nets, often facing an agonising and slow death.

In most countries this is something that fishermen are supposed to avoid, and in most countries it is either illegal or just unacceptable to process and profit from any cetacean 'by-catch'. Intriguingly, Japan, Norway and South Korea have laws which allow the landing, processing, and sale of these net-caught whales (Japan legalised this as recently as 2001).

Where other countries have low numbers of whales killed as by-catch in any one year (usually less than double figures), the numbers in these countries is often significantly greater. For example, in Japan in 2001 and 2002, a total of 188 minke whales were killed in nets, representing a fourfold increase immediately after it had become legal! Their meat would have been then legally processed and sold, suggesting rather forcefully that these catches are anything but unintentional. In South Korea, a net-caught whale in 2002 could fetch US$40,000 at auction. Indeed 'net whaling' has been a traditionally Japanese method of whaling since the 17th Century. It is not just the relatively small minkes killed in this way, 2002 also saw three humpback whales die in Japanese fishing nets.

Despite having no whaling programme, whale, dolphin and porpoise meat is readily available in South Korea

Less lethal alternatives

Of course, no one would suggest that the scientific study of whales and other cetaceans was a bad thing in principle. As we have already seen, there are enormous gaps in our cetacean knowledge – and more research on them is vital to help their conservation. Scientific study does not need to kill whales though, indeed there are many benefits of non-lethal research, most notably that you can make repeated observations of the same animals.

Let's just have a quick look at the list of research conducted by the Japanese whaling fleet, and see what options exist that don't involve killing whales.

Measurements are taken for body length, weight, age, growth, maturation, fertilisation and breeding. Much of this can be determined by repeated observations. Photographic records can be used to generate body length estimates, which can be extrapolated to work out weight. Repeated sighting and monitoring, such as regular observation and photographic records collected aboard regular whale-watching trips, is a better way to monitor age and maturation. Fertilisation and breeding information is also more meaningful when conducted non-lethally (rather than killing a whale to find out if it's pregnant!), particularly because mothers and calves can be observed together, and repeated observation can build up life history information on them both. For pregnancy, diet and stock structure information, tissue biopsies can be taken. This involves firing a dart at the animals to optain a sample for DNA or hormone analysis: certainly a better option for the whales than having a harpoon fired at them.

To track whales, there is the option of satellite tagging, which can provide a vivid picture in particular of migration routes between feeding and breeding grounds. Finally, there is the diet question – the somewhat unpleasant reality is that if anyone really wanted to know what a whale was eating, you can find out by examining their faeces. It's not pretty, but it's true, if they are serious about the science, they can do it without killing the whales.

Lastly, if you really, really, really, need some dead whales to examine, then the numerous stranded carcasses that wash up on our beaches every year provide ideal subjects. It's clear that the only real reason to conduct lethal 'scientific' whaling is to be able to continue whaling, not to further the scientific cause.

But there is some cause for optimism. In the wake of the renaissance of whales in the 70s, and the ban on commercial whaling in the 80s, a new industry emerged. It's an industry that now operates on every continent, and offers fantastic opportunities for studying whales, and is the only truly sustainable way to use them.

9

Gray whales often give whale watchers
a hands-on experience

9 | Whale watching

Making a splash

The first time I saw a humpback whale jump clear of the water and crash back down on the ocean surface with a thunderous splash, I exclaimed something in surprise that I'm too polite to reproduce in print. On a whale watching trip from Provincetown in Cape Cod we had already had some amazing views of enormous fin whales lunge-feeding on their sides at the ocean surface, small groups of harbour porpoises, and some close-up views of humpbacks with young calves. All of that was an amazing experience, but hadn't quite prepared me for the exhilaration of seeing a 30 tonne whale launch itself clear of the water right in front of us. I still gush about it to anyone who'll listen. The appeal of whale watching is not difficult to understand for anyone who has seen real live whales in the wild. The palpable excitement when seeing whales or dolphins is infectious, and makes grown-ups feel like kids again. Whether it's a glimpse of a speedy minke or fin whale slicing the ocean surface, or bow-riding dolphins, or a close encounter with a feeding or breaching humpback – it's a giddying experience.

Getting up close and personal with whales and dolphins is always inspiring. I'm a great believer in putting the camera away, and just enjoying the experience, as being able to relate it to people says much more than a blurry photo of a bit of fin can. And other people are much better at taking photographs than I am. It's not just the sight, and indeed the size of the whales that impresses; it's the sounds and smells too. You can hear the whistles of bow-riding common dolphins and the grunts and squeaks of a humpback calf as it splashes around on the surface whilst its mother dives to feed. Small shoaling bait fish make the ocean surface shimmer and fizz as they try to flee a fin whale chasing them underwater while larger fish jump clear of the water to escape the same beast. If you get close enough you get the smells too, from the waft of a misty blow catching

your face, to the overpowering fish-breath of a feeding fin whale right next to the boat.

Whale watching is now big business, with whale watching industries in over 90 countries worldwide, catering to over 10 million people each year. And the range of species and options open to the avid whale watcher is also huge. Of course the best place to see whales and dolphins is at sea, so most whale watching involves a boat trip. That can be on specially designed whale boats such as those in Cape Cod and other parts of New England, or converted wooden fishing boats like in parts of Iceland. In Alaska you can kayak with orcas, in South West England you can take a trip on an inflatable boat to see dolphins. In the Azores you have the chance of seeing big animals like sperm, fin and blues whales, as well as deep water specialists like some of the beaked whales in waters that used to be traditional whale killing grounds up until the IWC moratorium. In other places you don't even need to test your sea legs, and can watch whales from land. Shore-based whale watching takes place in California as the gray whales undertake their mammoth migrations along the coastline, in South Africa for Southern right whales, and in the Moray Firth in Scotland for bottlenose dolphins.

A whale of an industry

The growth of the whale watching industry has been phenomenal, and marks a sea change in the public's views on whales. They are no longer shot with harpoons and lances, but cameras and camcorders. Whale watching is now worth over US$1.25 billion worldwide annually. The industry is also perfectly suited for many of the coastal areas that were previously involved in whaling operations.

Image on preceding page:
An orca breaching in Alaska

Despite being spread all around the world's oceans, cetaceans are not evenly distributed. At different times of the year they are also found in different places. For the most part whales and dolphins follow their food, and good feeding grounds will depend on things like migrating shoals of small fish, and upwellings, mixing currents and shallow waters where plankton is plentiful. Sperm whales tend to be found on the edge of continental shelves, and other great whales make huge migrations to warm water breeding grounds, giving opportunities to catch them migrating, or as they aggregate to give birth to their calves. Unsurprisingly, that makes many former whaling nations and whaling ports ideally suited as bases for whale watching operations.

Most of the big whale species, including blue, fin, right, gray, humpback, sperm and minkes are whale watching subjects, as are many of the smaller toothed whales, from the awe-inspiring orcas all the way down to the tiny Hector's dolphin.

Not all cetaceans are 'good' to watch. The opportunity to get a view of whales and dolphins is limited to when they are at the water's surface. For some species this is a fleeting, and unspectacular glimpse. Other species, like most of the beaked whales live too far out to sea to see reliably or easily. The best options for whale watching are 'reliable' species, whose whereabouts and visibility can to some extent be predicted. For some this depends on their annual migrations, such as humpbacks passing the coast of Australia en route to and from the Antarctic, or gray whales hugging the shore of the Eastern seaboard as they migrate between Alaska and California. For others it is predictable aggregations to feed or breed, such as orcas following herring shoals into Norwegian fjords, or humpbacks feeding in the rich, shallow waters off Cape Cod.

Getting the hump

There are undoubtedly a few star species of whale-watching whales, and the undisputed global champion is the humpback whale. Its portly demeanour makes the humpback stand out amongst the rorquals, but it is the enormous irregularly-shaped flippers that clearly set it apart. They have the world record for the longest appendage of any vertebrate, and can be as long as 5 metres, or almost one third of the animal's total length. Given its prodigious flipper endowment and penchant for dining off the northeast US seaboard, it is quite fitting to know that the humpback's scientific name literally means 'big winged New Englander'. The other notable mentions in a humpback's CV are the amazingly elaborate underwater 'song' used in courtship, and the phenomenal migrations undertaken – which in some populations can involve journeys of over 8,000 kilometres between feeding and calving grounds.

For sheer entertainment value the humpback wins flippers down. It is an acrobatic whale, sometimes leaping clear of the water, and often engaging in tail and flipper slapping on the surface. It also kindly, if impolitely, eats with its mouth open at the surface, allowing some fantastic views of its gaping maw and expanded throat gulping down an enormous mouthful. If you're really lucky you'll get to see how they corral small prey by circling them and blowing bubbles, then coming up straight through the bait ball for a mouthful. It's the cetacean equivalent of successfully wrapping a decent mouthful of slippery spaghetti onto your fork. The humpback's name comes not from any hump, but from its characteristically arched back just before it dives. This arched back is both a blessing and a disappointment for the whale watchers – it conveniently warns you and your camera that the photographic money shot is about to happen, when the whale raises its tail fluke clear of the water, giving the archetypal image of a whale tail. The downside is that seeing the tail means the whale is diving down deep and won't resurface again for probably another 20 minutes or more.

On the spot

When feeding, some whales conveniently do it at the surface, but the sperm whale is very different. It dives very deep to capture its squiddy supper, and dives can last about an hour. The payback is that feeding sperm whales tend to come right back up where they go down, so all you need is a little patience. Indeed, all whale-watching requires patience and luck, for part of the thrill of seeing wild animals in their natural environment is that it is on their terms, and every whale watching trip will be unique.

In the years since the moratorium on commercial whaling was introduced, and in a world where whales have gone from being just another resource to plunder, to something worth saving, its whale watching that has been the big development. The industry has almost entirely grown up since the 1980s and since (and to a large extent because of) the commercial whaling ban, soon becoming an essential component of the tourist industry in many countries. In Iceland for example, it's estimated that over a third of visitors to the country go whale watching. The Icelandic Tourist Board reports that some 104,300 people went whale watching in Iceland in 2007, numbers that have shown a 500% increase in the past decade alone.[23] On top of a market for people making holiday choices specifically to include whale watching, it is increasingly also an industry that attracts other tourists whose trip was not for that reason. Whale watching can be a whole holiday or just part of one, it can be anything from a couple of hours to a couple of weeks, and it is one business that can truly claim to make sustainable use of the world's whales.

It probably doesn't need spelling out, but you can watch a whale many, many times, but kill it only once. In effect whale watching is the ultimate 'sustainable use' of whales, to use IWC terminology. The whale watching industry depends on whales, as did the whaling industry, but since only live whales are a marketable commodity to whale watchers, the former is much more proactively concerned with protecting its interests by protecting whales. There are some who argue that the two industries need not conflict, and need not overlap, so let's pause a while to see if that is true.

Every whale watcher's dream –
a humpback leaping clear of the water

A new confrontation

Whale watching depends on fairly regular and predictable encounters with whales. That means they need to operate in a way that does not adversely affect the whales. In some cases the mainstay of the whale watching industry is 'friendly' inquisitive whales that actively approach the whale watching vessels. This is true of gray whales in Baja, California, and minkes in Iceland and Scotland. In nearby Norway, you can't watch minke whales, but you can watch sperm whales and orcas. The minkes in Norwegian waters, where they are hunted still, are understandably shy of boats.

In Iceland the watching vs. whaling conflict quickly came to a head when 'scientific' whaling was restarted there in 2003. Despite assurances that there would be no impact on the areas important from whale watching, on top of whale watching tourists cancelling trips and pledging not to visit Iceland whilst it was whaling, whales were duly killed in some of the most important areas to the whale watching operators. The opposition to whaling in Iceland was new, but as with many countries around the world, there is a growing understanding of the importance of tourism to the economy. Tourism is now the second biggest industry in Iceland, and nature tourism including whale watching is one of its fastest-growing sectors. Tourists from Europe and North America are enticed to Iceland by the lure of a wild, natural unspoilt destination. Undoubtedly whaling has soured the appeal for many tourists, and has led the tourism industry internally to be one of the most vocal domestic critics of Icelandic whaling. As with other countries in the world, whaling in Iceland will end only when Iceland itself wants it to end, and the people of Iceland are now seriously considering the direct and indirect damage that the increasingly unnecessary industry of whaling will have on their economy and international standing. Any visitor to Reykjavik harbour will see for themselves the stark choice facing present day Iceland, an increasingly popular tourist destination for those from both sides of the North Atlantic. The proudly-maintained fleet of vast hulking grey whale catching vessels cast their ominous shadows on the busy whale watching tours ticket desk below.

Not on the whalers' agenda?

It is puzzling that whilst the debates within the IWC centre around the issue of continued whaling, whale watching, practised not only in more countries than whaling but also actually a thriving industry in more countries worldwide than are members of the IWC, is given little or no attention. It is clear that the proponents of whaling do not want whale watching to be properly considered as a sustainable use of whales, preferring instead that 'sustainable use' effectively means killing some.

As well as offering a lucrative and truly sustainable alternative industry based around local populations of whales, whale watching also offers an opportunity to increase both the knowledge of the tourists, and also add to the global scientific study of whale populations. A boat load of tourists are a captive and engaged audience eager to learn about the biology and conservation of the whales and indeed the wider ocean ecosystem they live in, from the plankton and fish that form the basis of the whales' menu, to the seabirds and seals around the vessel. It's also an opportunity to explain how the underwater geography, depth of water, and mixing currents affect food availability and make some areas good feeding grounds for whales. Even better, regular trips to watch whales also offer an opportunity to make useful scientific observations too. Recording sightings, sounds, locations, numbers, behaviour and information on individual animals can all help to add to the global scientific knowledge of whale populations. With migrating and long-lived species, and particularly depleted populations, this can offer vital information for the ongoing conservation of whales. In some species individual whales can be identified. In some this is a matter of distinguishing marks on dorsal fins and the like but in the humpback this information is even more useful and readily available. Each individual has unique markings on the underside of its tail fluke. They are as recognisable as human fingerprints, allowing photo identification to be made of these whales at sea.

Contributing to a global catalogue of identified individuals, information can then be gathered on the family relationships, migration patterns and feeding grounds of individuals and populations, leading to a better understanding of humpbacks. Good identification of humpback whales can now even be made from computerised databases of photographic records, thanks to the pooling of information from around the world. In the North Atlantic alone there is a photographic inventory of more than 6,000 whales, thanks to collaboration between biologists and whale watching operations. Even better, these individuals can keep giving us new data to add, as they can be repeatedly monitored when encountered. For some individuals there are now decades worth of sightings data. By contrast, taking a scientific sample by explosive harpoon would only give a snapshot of the humpback's life and an estimated age that would say nothing about the animal's life history.

It's not only humpback whales who can be identified and studied in this way; the same is true of blue whales which have unique patterning on their flanks visible as they break the surface. Gray whales also have unique markings, and can be recognised as individual animals by them. Closely-studied populations of orcas and bottlenose dolphins can also be identified from photographic study. It's possible to identify individuals of these and other species when they have scars or colouration that is unusual. At the most extreme level, there is a completely white humpback whale called 'Migaloo' that has become a bit of a celebrity in Australian waters. Yet whilst whale watching has undoubtedly created some celebrated stars, other less-photogenic, and less-accessible cetaceans have been quietly disappearing from our seas and rivers. Their fate is not helped by the perpetually polarised and paralysed nature of whaling politics.

BYE-BYE BAIJI

10

Dodo

10 | Bye-bye baiji

Slipping away unnoticed

The 59th meeting of the IWC in Alaska was the first IWC meeting to ever preside over the extinction of a species of cetacean. In 2007 the Baiji (**Lipotes vexillifer**) a dolphin from China, was declared extinct. What was perhaps even more remarkable about the event was that it seemed to pass by almost un-noticed.

As far back as 1990, the writer Douglas Adams (who famously gave a free-falling sperm whale a cameo role in his **Hitchhiker's Guide to the Galaxy**) searched in vain for the baiji on a trip to China, documented in his book **Last Chance to See**.[24] Even then, the only baiji to be found in the murky waters of the Yangtze was a solitary captive specimen in an aquarium, called Qi-Qi.

True, maybe the baiji had inevitably been heading towards oblivion for a long time, but a unique species was wiped out and, with the exception of environmental and conservation groups, virtually no one batted a particularly-concerned eyelid. This is surely a damning indictment of the current global priorities facing whale conservation: a species disappears forever, yet the politicians and bureaucrats spend most of their time treading water and trying to save face or secure minor victories over the future of commercial whaling.

The baiji was a fish-eating river dolphin confined to the Yangtze river basin. Despite official protection since 1949, the baiji's numbers declined as its habitat did. There are also river dolphins in the Ganges, and in the Amazon, where the better-known boto (**Inia geoffrensis**) actually swims amongst the flooded rainforest trees. These are very specialist animals with long beaks and sharp teeth, and very isolated populations. Indeed, being confined to brackish and fresh water habitats around which humans are increasingly encroaching does not seem to be the most forward-thinking evolutionary strategy. Rivers the world over tend to act like conveyor belts for humans to dump unpleasant things into, both directly and indirectly. They also serve as thoroughfares for traffic, and the Yangtze is no different. Heavily polluted and very cloudy water characterizes the river – although the visibility itself would not have been an issue for the echolocating baiji. But of course any animal that used sound to 'see' would have been at a severe disadvantage when the river got increasingly noisier through man-made noises, like boat engines. Pollution has taken a heavy toll on much of the life in the Yangtze, and most of the fish that would have been the baiji's prey have disappeared. Add that to entanglement in fishing nets, the effects of pollution in their food, and its effects on the baiji themselves... and it was a world that changed too fast to allow the baiji to cope.

Extinction: a tale of two pigeons

Extinctions are, of course, nothing new. The Atlantic gray whale is extinct, a process that was at the very least speeded up by human intervention. But that was over two and a half centuries ago, and we can perhaps be excused for not having known better, back then.

Among the catalogue of famous extinctions, there are two birds that are no longer with us that are worthy of a mention – for their predicaments can be compared with some of our cetacean friends. If you ask any child to name an extinct animal, the one that is likely to be top of the list (even beating velociraptors!) is the dodo (**Raphus cucullatus**): a large flightless pigeon that used to live on the island of Mauritius in the Indian Ocean. Whilst often ridiculed for its perceived oddness, the dodo had evolved perfectly well for its habitat – it had no predators to fear, and no need to fly. It had not however, been prepared for the arrival of humans, and the ravaging bands of cat, rat, monkey, and pig followers they brought with them. Easy-to-kill dodos were treated as a somewhat gamey, but handy source of food. Direct persecution, deforestation and the destruction of eggs by man's marauding mammalian entourage, meant that within only about 70 years of its discovery by Dutch sailors in 1598, the dodo was dead, it was deceased, it was an ex-pigeon.

The tales of discovery of new limitless resources that were then plundered are global. Sailors after bigger or richer prizes often wreaked havoc on other species en route, without either consideration of the impact they were having, or concern for the disappearance of the species. The late great auk, and Steller's sea cow provided brief but notable bonanzas before their inconvenient extinctions sent mankind looking elsewhere.

The other bird worth pausing to consider is the passenger pigeon (**Ectopistes migratorius**): a North American bird that was once the most numerous bird on earth. It travelled in enormous flocks that blocked out the sun, estimated to contain up to 2 billion birds, and could literally take days to pass overhead. When an animal is so ubiquitous you can understand that every individual hunter would never have considered it possible to even make a dent in their numbers. But they did. Relentless hunting over decades reduced the passenger pigeon numbers disastrously, and they were extinct in the wild by 1900. Then there was only one left, a female called Martha in Cincinnati Zoo. Her death in 1914 marked the extinction of a species that was once so numerous it was impossible to comprehend had, incomprehensibly, been annihilated.

As well as these 'famous' extinctions, there are also many animals that are now, or have been in the past reduced to perilously low numbers and the brink of extinction, many of them familiar species to us: elephant seals, sea otters, giant pandas, and white rhinos. Some of those still teeter on the brink; others have recovered, showing that protection for even grossly depleted stocks can work. For some it may be too late – on the Galapágos Island of Pinta is one solitary remaining member of a subspecies of giant tortoise, his name, rather aptly is Lonesome George. Ironically, Pacific whalers used to make use of these giant tortoises as a readily-available, easy-to-catch and long-lasting supply of meat – they could be kept alive without food or water in the ship's hold for many months. Many other species such as golden toads, and Spix's macaws now exist only in the protection of zoological collections, in the hope that one day they may be successfully reintroduced to a suitable habitat.

These are cautionary tales, for it is clearly possible to irrevocably damage a species' ability to exist by persecuting it if it is restricted in range, like the baiji, the vaquita, gray whales, or narwhals and it is equally possible to do irreversible damage by simply depleting 'limitless' wide-ranging stocks too much. Remember the tales of how many whales there were each time a new stock was discovered, and the boom and bust cycle of species after species and area after area? Coupled with other, less tangible, and often less visible, impacts – our impact on cetaceans and the waters in which they live is cumulatively a lot greater than we think.

Whale populations today

We've had a global ban on commercial whaling in effect now for over 20 years, and in that time, yes, some species have shown signs of recovery. Some of these are those that have been protected longest (many nominally protected for decades before the moratorium), but it's clear that some species and populations, such as the Californian gray whale, have shown amazing resilience and luck in the face of relentless persecution. There are still enormous gaps in what we know, our estimates for most whale populations are sketchy or tentative at best, and for some species, like the ocean dwelling species of beaked whales, we know very little. In fact some of them have never even been seen alive.

Other species of the better-known whales are facing mixed fortunes. On one side of the Pacific, gray whales numbers have recovered dramatically, with the Californian population now believed to be almost as large as it was pre-exploitation. These whales now support a thriving whale watching industry too. Western gray whales are however in a dire state, the total population is estimated at less than 100 individuals, of which only a couple of dozen at most are believed to be females of breeding age. They are under threat from many human impacts – from fishing nets and noise disturbance, to oil and gas exploration – and every single gray whale lost from that population is a matter of grave concern for the future viability of the Western grays as a whole.

Southern right whales (**Balaena australis**) seem to be doing okay, and they are also supporting a healthy whale watching trade in South Africa. But North Atlantic right whales aren't faring quite so well, with ship strikes proving to be a major source of mortality for an already distressed population, believed to number less than 300 animals. Blue whale numbers have yet to show any significant increase. In truth it will probably be a long, long time, even in ideal conditions, for the world's whale populations to recover, and conditions at present are far from ideal. Not only are the oceans degraded, overexploited and polluted but they face a phenomenal threat from the impacts of global climate change. And the truth is that for these other impacts on the whale populations, we really don't have an accurate understanding of just how bad things are.

At the other end of the size scale some of the world's smallest cetaceans are under immediate threat. The diminutive vaquita, a Mexican porpoise, harbour porpoise populations in the North and Baltic Seas, and New Zealand's Hector's dolphins all face a precarious future as a result of being routinely caught as by-catch in fishing nets.

And just to make things more confusing...

Indeed, the matter of knowing the populations is even more uncertain than it may at first appear. For sanity's sake I have tried to keep information on whale species simple; but it really isn't. The truth is, as well as uncertainty on population numbers, there is also huge uncertainty over how many whale species, and subspecies (let alone separate populations) there are. For example, the populations of North and South right whales is separate, but are the North Atlantic right whales and North Pacific right whales separate species or not? And then what happens if the Arctic ice melts? The same is true of the distinct

Vaquita

Western and Californian gray whales. The relatively humble minke whale is believed to be up to three separate species, in the northern and southern hemispheres, with a 'pygmy' species too. Some authorities are convinced there is also a 'pygmy' blue whale. And that's just a snapshot of the baleen whales: toothed whales are equally confusing. Are offshore orcas and bottlenose dolphins separate species or subspecies to those that live in resident coastal groups? Then there are the elusive beaked whales, which we know so little about that many of the guide book representations are more like police photo-fits.

We can't even be sure of what the pre-exploitation populations of whales were like, and centuries of poorly-recorded information have made it a quagmire of conflicting 'facts'. Whales were recorded by the number of barrels of oil they produced, rather than size or species; species themselves were inconsistently identified; catches were under-reported and it wasn't just Meincke who over-exaggerated the size of animals that were caught! Work is underway now to try and get a better understanding of some of this from DNA evidence, but given how few of some types of whales are encountered, this may take a very, very long time.

What does all that uncertainty and confusion mean, though? Well, the truth is we don't know, but it should make us more precautionary in our approach to whale numbers, as they may be much more fragmented and depleted than we currently think.

Given how much we don't know about these animals, it's difficult to assess the true damage we are doing. What seems to be abundantly clear though is that the world over, legislation to protect whales, dolphins and porpoises is failing, and the world in which they are living is getting increasingly more dangerous.

In the time it has taken to write this book a new species of cetacean has been officially named. We have lost the baiji, but we have discovered the bufeo, or Bolivian river dolphin (**Inia boliviensis**) which was only declared officially as a separate species from the boto in April 2008. The bufeo hopefully faces a brighter future than the baiji, as the Bolivian government has quickly adopted it as mascot for the country's track record on conservation.

11

Southern right whale goes human watching

11 | The bigger picture

Whose whales are they anyway?

Arguably, you and I have as much right to the whales in the high seas of the Southern Ocean as anyone standing behind a harpoon gun. The problem for whales, and other animals that inhabit the global commons of our high seas, is that it's a free-for-all. Because they belong to no one country, it's a grab-them-while-you-can trolley dash. Our oceans represent the problem known as the 'Tragedy of the Commons' on a vast scale. The big problem is there is no adequate policing of our high seas, although, to be fair, matters aren't much better in national waters or Exclusive Economic Zones either. Around the world ineffective legislation is failing our oceans, and the priority remains one of exploitation, as if crashes in populations of hunted sea creatures the world round had taught us nothing.

It's difficult to imagine in today's depleted seas what our oceans would have been like before we dipped our greedy toes into them, although it must have been something like the image that presented itself to whalers of old each time they discovered new untouched areas of ocean where whales abounded. One of the arguments that is repeatedly used today, as a valid 'scientific' reason as to why we might have to control populations of whales is this: 'whales eat fish'. If this wasn't so pernicious and insidious it might be funny. The argument is increasingly stated as fact, and is often trotted out as a reason why a small and/or developing nation has joined the IWC (at Japan's behest, and voting with them!) because they are concerned that the whales are taking all their fish. Labelling cetaceans as competing predators endangering our fish stocks is also a handy way of getting around any notions of a 'precautionary approach' to impacts on them.

Yes, some whales do eat fish, although those that are being hunted in the Southern Ocean don't! I think the response I'm most tempted to make is, 'so what?' Of course the underlying

message that that is supposed to convey is, 'the whales are eating OUR fish'. This stems from the same idea that somehow we have an inalienable right to take what we want from the planet, irrespective of the effects that has on other species, or the long-term implications. It is a remarkably blinkered viewpoint. Stop for a second and think which species has more claim as natural ocean-going predators: humans or whales?

Scaremongers and fishmongers

It's not just whales that get this thrown at them – seals, and seabirds do too. Often with scaremongering extrapolations of just how much fish they are eating worldwide, and how that compares to human consumption. The logic seems to be, if it wasn't for these pesky animals taking all of our fish, we'd have plenty to go round. So let's have a quick look at that logic. Assuming we have some absolute ownership of the fish in the sea, then we presumably should do our best to stop anything else eating them. What eats most fish? Why, bigger fish. To badly bastardise a famously anonymous poem – **Little fish, have bigger fish, that swim around to bite them, and bigger fish have bigger fish, and so ad infinitum.**

So presumably we should kill them? Well, in effect, we've done a pretty good job of that already. The amounts of large predatory fish in our oceans (including culinary favourites like cod, tuna, swordfish, and marlin) are currently languishing at about 10% of their numbers before industrialised fishing,[25] which took off in earnest in the mid 20th Century. That means that increasingly we have to catch smaller fish to get our fix of ocean protein. In the North Sea the average size of a cod landed in the 1960s was 1.62 metres long. That had shrunk to 0.46 metres in 1996.

That means we are taking increasingly smaller and younger animals. This has an adverse impact on the ability of those

Image on preceding page:
Oil and gas developments pose a very
real threat to Western gray whales

populations to survive and replenish, because bigger fish are more likely to be sexually mature (very helpful if you want baby fishes in years to come) and also lay more eggs (therefore having more potential baby fishes, and giving a better chance of survival to at least some of them). Also, taking predatory fish out of the system means that there are other critters that they may have eaten which might be more numerous and feasting on the eggs and baby fishes and making it even worse. We cannot assume that removing predatory species will have a simple knock-on effect, or that the 'unpredated' animals will be ours for the taking. Where overfishing has had its most dramatic effects, we have seen fundamental and unpredictable shifts in the make-up of ecosystems. In some cases, crustaceans like crabs have come to dominate, in others, jellyfish.

A study in 2004 by the University of British Columbia concluded that there was actually very little crossover in the species eaten by whales and humans; more evidence that the apparent 'conflict' is in fact just a bit of creative campaigning designed to justify killing some whales.[26]

I have a colleague who likens the blaming of whales for eating all the fish to blaming woodpeckers for deforestation. It is patently nonsensical. Yes, there is a highly developed mammal destroying global fish stocks, and it's about time we accepted the blame.

Fishing – how not to do it

In centuries past, when whales, seals, sea otters, seabirds, sharks, tuna, and cod were all much more plentiful, so were the fish and other animals they fed on. Predatory animals always exist in smaller numbers than their prey, and are – to an extent – limited by its availability. The only animal that really upsets that balance is us; we can overfish, overhunt, and overexploit (as we have repeatedly proved), because we have so far been supremely resourceful at switching to another target when one disappears.

The example of international fisheries should not be an excuse to persecute whales or any other animals, it should be a wake-up call to just how badly wrong we have got it. In theory, living things are renewable 'resources'. They are replaceable, given the ability and time to do so. However, any fishing (or any other form of hunting, for that matter) by humans assumes that there is an 'excess' of ocean creatures there for us to take, that can be skimmed off the population without doing any harm. Fish, as a rule, grow and mature more quickly than whales. They also have much bigger numbers of progeny, so in theory, should be a much more renewable resource: female cod of about 1.27 metres long can produce about 9 million eggs.

Cod is the perfect example. Like passenger pigeons, the cod of the Grand Banks in the northwest Atlantic were deemed so numerous that nothing could ever dent their numbers. When the fisheries were first discovered, the cod were said to be so numerous you could walk on their backs, and fish them simply by dropping a basket in the water. In the Massachusetts State House, in Boston, a wooden model of a 'sacred' cod hangs above the debating chamber, a gift from cod fishermen to remind its members never to forget the importance of the fish to the region. Mere decades after the expansion of industrialised fisheries for cod in this region the stock crashed – becoming commercially (if not biologically) extinct in 1992. Ignoring years of scientific advice warning of imminent stock collapse, fishing had carried on. The disappearance of the cod meant that 30,000 fishermen were put out of a job in the process. Almost 20 years later the fishery has still not recovered.

Nor have we even learned the direct lesson from the cod fishery. Cod in the North Sea is also in a precarious state, yet repeatedly politicians ignore scientific advice and set quotas for fisheries that are totally unsustainable, and in complete defiance of scientific advice. Then, as soon as there are any signs of even very small improvements in stock numbers, there is enormous pressure on politicians from the fishing industry clamouring to immediately increase fishing effort. Precaution is cast aside in favour of short-term political and fishing interests: after all fish don't vote, but fishermen do.

Globally there are enormous parallels between the fishing and whaling industry. Species after species and region after region has been fished out. Advances in technology and the lack of familiar and local species have driven fishermen to target species and areas never-before deemed worthwhile. In the same way as the sei and minke whales were turned to by a whaling industry desperate to maintain catches after hunting out the giants, so too do the world's fishing fleets target ever smaller species of fish, at ever lower levels of the food web. We fish small fish to turn into meal to feed caged fish, pigs, and chickens. The same is now also happening to krill. So rather than whales eating OUR fish, we're actually increasingly working our way down the food web and taking theirs.

The statistics are appalling: globally three-quarters of fish stocks are either fully exploited, over-exploited or trashed,[27] and 65% of all fisheries exploited since the 1950s have collapsed.[28] Some scientists suggest that if we keep going as we are, then all the world's commercial fisheries will have disappeared by 2050.[29]

Fishing is not only a perfect example of oceanic mismanagement, but it is also responsible for direct and indirect threats to whales. Cetaceans are killed by entanglement in fishing gear, and have their food supply depleted by overfishing.

By-catch

By-catch is the polite way of saying 'casualty of fishing'. When it refers to commercial fish species which are under size or over quota, it is more commonly known as 'discards'. By-catch however can be almost any ocean living creature, from bottom dwelling sea urchins and shellfish, to sharks, turtles, albatrosses, and all the way up to large whales. The species at risk vary depending on where and when the fishery is, and what fishing gear is used. Some fisheries are incredibly wasteful, with trawl fisheries for plaice and shrimp often having more than 70% of the catch as non-target species. Other fisheries have a devastating effect on particular species, such as long line fisheries for

Patagonian toothfish, which use lines many kilometres long with hundreds of baited hooks, and are responsible for the deaths of an estimated 10,000 albatrosses annually – many of which are now critically endangered. It is a monumental waste of life by indiscriminate and lazy (but presumably profitable) fishing methods. It has been conservatively estimated that 300,000 whales, dolphins and porpoises are killed by direct human activity every year – the overwhelming majority of them by being entangled in fishing gear.[30] In some cases the sheer numbers are staggering, especially in the light of more selective methods of fishing gear that are available to the fishermen. In other cases the by-catch is causing a direct threat to the existence of species or populations of whales, dolphins and porpoises. Given that we don't fully understand separate social structures and populations of cetaceans, it's quite likely we're doing a lot more damage than we realise.

Western gray whales are occasionally caught and killed in fishing nets in the seas around Japan, and with numbers so low, every single mortality poses a real threat to a population on the brink. In New Zealand the survival of Hector's dolphins (**Cephalorhyncus hectori**), and particularly the North Island's sub-population known as 'Maui dolphins' is at risk from deaths caused in fishing nets. In the Baltic Sea, an already impoverished population of harbour porpoises is at threat from static 'gill nets'. In the nearby North Sea it has been estimated that 8,000 harbour porpoises a year could be being killed by these nets. In the Gulf of California the tiny vaquita (**Phocoena sinus**), a porpoise whose Spanish name means 'little cow', is endangered by fishing nets for totoaba, a fish that can be as big or even bigger than the vaquita. Unless the fishing nets disappear, it's likely that the vaquita will.

Image on facing page:
Common dolphin killed as by-catch
in the English Channel

If this destruction was happening on land, instead of out at sea and out-of-sight, it would cause a global outrage. In his wonderfully shocking book on the parlous state of global fishing, **The End of the Line,**[31] Charles Clover vividly imagines what indiscriminate trawling would look like if transferred to the African plains, and killed elephants, giraffes, cheetahs and wildebeest. Perhaps it would be more appropriate to take the analogy to the streets of our towns and cities, or the committees of politicians who let this go on. Would we be so non plussed then, I wonder? The vast majority of the cetaceans caught as by-catch are the smaller species like dolphins and porpoises.

Pair-trawling is a method of fishing stringing one very large net between two fishing boats. Generally the nets are in the water for hours on end, scouring the sea for straggling fish. Any cetacean trapped in them suffers a prolonged and agonising death, being unable to surface for air. Dolphins can literally rip their own muscles apart, break their beaks and teeth, and slice off chunks of flipper trying to break free.

I've seen at first hand dolphins freshly discarded from pair-trawler nets in the English Channel. In an attempt to ensure the carcasses would sink and disappear the fishermen had slit the bodies from belly to throat; the bodies were still warm, and one of them was still lactating. Of course, a dead female that was lactating means that somewhere there was an orphaned baby dolphin, that was also dead, or very soon would be. Aboard the **Esperanza** we were confronting pair-trawlers targeting bass, an increasingly fashionable fish. It is also caught by a local hand-line fishery, which has no associated by-catch, and yields better quality fish. Unsurprisingly, the local fishermen are not keen on the pair-trawling vessels, which target the bass as they aggregate to spawn, thereby threatening the future of the fish population, and the livelihoods of local fishermen as well as the dolphins. All cetaceans are supposed to be 'protected species' under European Union law. Yet every year thousands are killed in nets in European waters and are 'excused' because they are the accidental cost of a perfectly legal fishing industry. Even in the face of a clear dolphin by-catch problem, and a viable alternative, politicians have failed to take effective action on pair-trawling for bass, and dolphins are still dying in the English Channel as a result of indiscriminate fishing methods.

Whilst on the **Rainbow Warrior** in Iceland, just after they had announced their plans to restart 'scientific' whaling in 2003, I heard a fisherman brag that between his two vessels he caught and killed about 400 dolphins a year. Most of them he threw back in, some he claimed to give to people to eat. The shy and retiring harbour porpoise is particularly at risk from fixed nets, and often carcasses are found washed up onshore around the UK mutilated as fishermen have had to hack off fins, tails or heads to save their nets, or they have ropes tied round their tails which have been used to winch them overboard. Whilst few people would disagree that this is a morally reprehensible and unacceptable situation, the fact is that most people don't get to know about it because it's out at sea, and out of sight.

Serving no porpoise

Just as an example of how ineffective legislation currently is at protecting cetaceans, even against fisheries with a known by-catch problem, we should look at the European Commission's Regulation of 2004. This law was specifically introduced to attempt to reduce the by-catch of small cetaceans in European fisheries. Static nets, like gill nets, pose a problem for cetaceans. But there is a solution – or there should be. The Regulation required fishermen using these nets to fix acoustic devices (called 'pingers') to their nets to try and alert and ward off porpoises in particular. Tests have shown promising results that these devices work in deterring the animals from the nets, although conservationists understandably questioned the long-term and widespread use of anything that created extra noise in the oceans. But the issue is academic. Three years after the Regulation was supposed to come into force pingers are not being used, because there are problems with them, and fishermen refuse to use them. That means that in fisheries with known by-catch problems, and with legislation that is supposed to try and address it, precisely nothing is being done, except some shrugging by politicians. The only realistic way to stop by-catch of a protected species in the absence of any technological solution is to ban the fishing method – but again, porpoises don't vote either.

Toxic trash

Globally we are persistently filling our oceans with all manner of unpleasant things – from chemicals used in industry and farming, to oil spills, radioactive waste, and the appalling legacy of our own litter and rubbish. Pollution can be a very obvious and visible problem (as it is when there is a catastrophic oil spill), or a deadly yet invisible one. The Pacific Ocean is home to an enormous 'trash vortex', where currents conspire to concentrate humanity's plastic waste in a vast swirling floating trash carpet the size of Texas (and growing daily with discarded fast-food wrappers, and over-zealously hit golfballs). It's estimated that in areas there are six kilograms of floating plastic for every kilogram of plankton, not a good ratio for any whales that eat small plankton by the enormous mouthful. Smaller cetaceans, particularly those that like to eat squid, are also at the mercy of the currently fashionably unfashionable plastic bags, which do a passing impression of a tasty invertebrate when submerged, but are much less digestible.

Because of their place in the ecosystem, and their blubbery physique, cetaceans are particularly prone to accruing large levels of toxic chemicals like mercury, and so-called 'persistent' pollutants from agricultural run-off, and industrial processes. The bad news is that ocean mammals continue to add to their toxin level as they age. A heavy toxic load can cause problems with the nervous system, and affect behaviour. However even if there is no apparent immediate effect on the animal, it significantly reduces its ability to handle disease and infection, as well as diminishes its ability to reproduce, or cope with other stresses. The big losers on toxin level are the toothed whales, with Norwegian Arctic orcas holding the dubious honour of the record levels of toxicity including pesticides and flame retardants – substances clearly not produced in the Arctic.

Disorienting decibels

Another pernicious by-product of humans is noise. At first that may seem somewhat insignificant and inconsequential but we need to think what ramifications that has for cetaceans, to whom sound is the primary sense.

Dead harbour porpoise washed up on
a beach in Cornwall, UK

As well as an increase in general noise in the oceans from more vessels (with bigger engines); underwater cables and pipelines; offshore industry dredging and drilling, there are phenomenal sounds generated by military sonar and weapons testing which can have a direct and devastating effect on individual animals. As background noise increases, communication between ocean-dwelling mammals becomes increasingly difficult – an issue made worse if the individuals are sparsely populated, widely distributed or depleted by whaling! Deep-diving toothed cetaceans like sperm whales and beaked whales are at a particular risk from very loud noises such as those generated in oil and gas exploration, and by military sonar and explosives.

These noises, frequently over 200 decibels, can disorient and even completely deafen animals, and is believed to be responsible for causing mass strandings of these species such as the stranding of 17 cetaceans (of three different species) in the Bahamas in 2000, understood to be a result of US Naval sonar used in a military exercise. In the first few months of 2008, an unusually large number of whale deaths of different species have been witnessed on the west coast of Scotland and Ireland, suspected to be the result of UK Naval sonar exercises taking place in the area. Recent research suggests that this military noise could be responsible for causing these deep-diving whales to surface too quickly – causing symptoms of decompression (like the 'bends') that do not seem to happen naturally in these species.

Strike out
A direct and palpable impact on the slower species of large whales is being hit by ships. Ship strikes cause damage from the propellers, or just the bulk of the vessel hitting the animal at speed. I probably don't need to elaborate that these can be particularly bloody and gory encounters. The question may arise as to why the whales get hit in the first place, but we should remember that these big animals are not familiar with anything in the ocean big enough to do them damage... and a whale

Krill

that already knows that a ship strike is a dangerous thing is likely to already be a severely injured whale. A few species are at particular risk from shipping, and they are often those that are already depleted from centuries of whaling such as gray and right whales: slow-moving whales that didn't manage to avoid harpoon-wielders in rowing boats. For Western grays and North Atlantic rights any individual whale lost is a severe blow to a precarious population, yet for both of these populations losses from ship strikes continue to pose a very real threat.

Eating disorder

Clearly, getting enough food is a crucial issue for any animal, and whales are no exception. The distribution of whales, including some phenomenal seasonal movements and migration distances, is influenced by where their prey is. Of course there are natural fluctuations in food availability, much the same as there are good and bad harvests, but human activities are making the situation much more problematic. As well as the impacts of human-induced climate change, industry and pollution our fishing is depleting the seas of food for whales, dolphins and porpoises. Increasingly this is becoming a direct conflict, as we fish out the bigger species and move further down the food web, the ocean creatures we are rapaciously harvesting on an industrial scale are those that the whales depend on.

Often the sea creatures that are caught in vast numbers are small, unappetising species like sandeel or blue whiting which are not destined for direct human consumption – but are turned into oil and fish meal, being fed to livestock like pigs and chickens, and ironically, to farmed fish. This is reaching a crunch point in the Southern Ocean, where one of the world's fastest growing fishing sectors is targeting the vast swarms of krill that are the basis of the entire Antarctic food web and, as we know, the favoured food of the whales.

Hotting up

The single most pressing issue facing the world is global climate change. This is already having an impact on ocean temperatures, and the polar ice caps. It will also likely result in fundamental changes to ocean currents, and salinity, as well as sea levels. The impacts for cetaceans are by no means certain – but they don't look good. Both of the polar regions are particularly important for whales; the Southern Ocean is a vast feeding ground for most of the world's baleen whales and the Arctic is a unique environment that grays, bowheads, belugas and narwhals depend on. Other species already survive in limited geographical ranges – such as the vaquita, gray whales, and river dolphins. For them, changes in sea temperature and the availability of food could prove irreversible. It's likely that suitable geographic conditions will not be available (and we humans are already taking up lots of space on the planet as it is, leaving less room for displaced whale species to move into) so that it's not a straightforward issue of just moving a few miles north or south.

It also doesn't necessarily follow that cetaceans will be able to cope with changed ecosystems. This is particularly true for the baleen species, like grays and humpbacks, which migrate vast distances but depend on a reliable food supply in their feeding grounds.

Krill is a good example of how these issues can be compounded. Not only are krill populations already showing signs of enormous decreases because of the loss of sea ice (where they typically feed on algae around the edges) by as much as 80% since the 1970s,[32] but now they are under pressure from commercial fishing interests. Clearly neither story is good news for the baleen whales that feed almost exclusively on krill in the Southern Ocean, and taken together they could well spell disaster.

Clearly the stresses affecting the world's whales, dolphins and porpoise are many, varied and cumulative, and the future for many of them looks fraught with danger. Most of the issues I've just mentioned are vast, some are solvable, albeit only with concerted international action, and others like climate change, we can only hope to now have a limiting effect on. But the fact is we have to do what we can to limit our impact on the wider environment, and ensure it can be as robust as possible to face the challenges of the future. The first step in doing that is doing what we can easily do now.

Trapped in nets and unable to reach
the surface for air, dolphins, porpoises
and whales face long agonising deaths

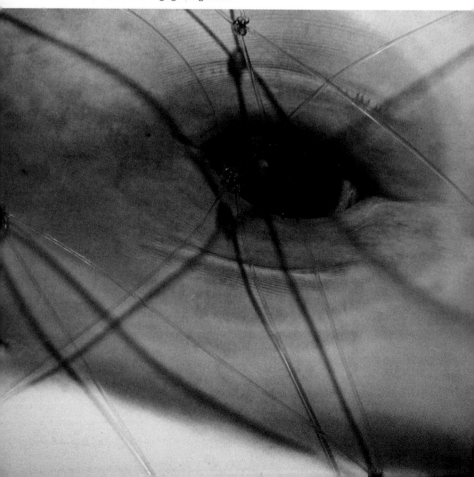

12

12 | What we need to do

The wrong focus?

In many ways whaling is no longer the biggest threat to the world's whale populations, but it is certainly the one that takes up all the media coverage, and the political and diplomatic effort.

Nowadays approximately 25,000 cetaceans are still hunted and killed around the world every year. Of these, about 2,500 are what we call Great whales (those regulated by the IWC). Unregulated hunts for small cetaceans like pilot whales, dolphins and Dall's porpoises still take place and account for the majority of cetaceans killed directly each year. Much of this is still done by drive-hunting, corralling groups of animals into shallow bays where they are herded into the shallows so they can be killed. Smaller numbers of whales allocated as 'Aboriginal Subsistence Whaling' account for the remainder.

But we also know that globally we are also killing hundreds of thousands of cetaceans every year in fishing gear. Hundreds of others, often from critically endangered populations, are killed or fatally wounded by ship strikes. Countless others are affected by pollution, many killed directly by our waste and others have their survival endangered by the build-up of pollutants that affect their ability to fight off illness or reproduce effectively. Yet others are affected by noise in our oceans; for some this means they are deafened and unable to communicate, or deterred from areas that may well be important for breeding or feeding, for others the impact is more direct with naval sonar being thought responsible for causing deep-diving whales to suffer injury, disorientation, and to become stranded onshore.

Image on facing page:
To whale or to watch a whale? The ominous crows' nests of whaling vessels overshadow Reykjavik's whale watching industry

Habitat for whales and dolphins is also lost through coastal developments in tourist destinations with an apparently ever-growing demand for purpose-built palm-tree shaped island resorts, and coastal concentrations of land-based pollution are particularly problematic for cetaceans that live in large river basins and coastal waters.

Global fisheries are both removing food sources and fundamentally changing marine ecosystems on which whales, dolphins and porpoises depend. Much of this is not even destined for direct consumption, but rather to make fish meal or oil to feed to livestock and farmed fish. Finally, global climate change is already affecting our oceans, and having an impact on the distribution of species. Quite what impact this will have on the world's remaining whale populations is uncertain, but accelerated human-induced climate change in already polluted and degraded oceans is unlikely to be good news for populations that are already impoverished and weakened. What will the impacts be on available food and habitats? On currents and sea temperatures? For disease resistance and reproductive ability? Given its potentially catastrophic impact on entire ocean ecosystems, climate change could yet wreak more havoc on whales and other ocean species than any other human effect.

It all adds up
None of these issues exist in isolation either – they have cumulative impacts on individual animals, entire species, and entire ecosystems. Some of these interactions we can already imagine – such as malnourished animals, or those with higher toxin levels having lower tolerance of disease and lower reproductive success. Many other interactions, particularly in light of global climate change and fundamental changes to ecosystems we can only speculate at.

The huge list of problems facing the world's whales mean that we need to move beyond polarized arguments on commercial whaling and focus instead on the very real conservation needs of the world's cetaceans. And that will require some radical and far-reaching action if we are serious in wanting to preserve not only our whales, dolphins, and porpoises, but also the oceans that they depend on. To protect long-lived species like the larger whales, and diminished populations of other species, that will take time, and effective measures. Despite decades of protection from whaling, many species show little or no real recovery. Blue whales, reduced to an estimated one per cent of their pre-whaling abundance have yet to show significant signs of recovery. North Atlantic right whale numbers are languishing in the low hundreds, every ship collision pushing the population further towards oblivion; the relict population of Western gray whales is beset by pollution, habitat loss, oil and gas developments, and entanglement in fishing gear. Other species like fin, and humpback are a mere shadow of their former numbers and we don't really have a good idea of how numerous or resilient they are.

As we increasingly fracture and geographically confine populations – just how resilient will they be to cope? Recent studies have shown that the highly-migratory Californian gray whales are already showing changes in the extent and timing of their migrations as a result of changing climate and availability of prey. Temperature changes may necessitate a migration north or south, but that could lead to conflict and competition with other species, or other human activities. It may also be the case that there is no suitable habitat where the more comfortable temperatures are (the undersea geology may be wrong), or because there is no mixing of waters or edge of ice shelf, there may be inadequate food supplies. Another insidious threat we can already see happening is that nations are already making 'grabs' for the right to develop, exploit and lay claim to areas of the Arctic and Antarctic. The effects of climate change are more pronounced at the poles, and nations are pre-empting the reduction in ice cover making these areas more accessible for extractive industries in particular. Both polar sea areas are crucial feeding grounds for many species of whales, some of them may well have nowhere else to go.

What's needed

1) The IWC & international agreements

The moratorium on commercial whaling needs to be permanent. Not only has commercial whaling never led to sustainable takes of whales, it has seriously depleted some species that still haven't recovered. On top of that the world that we and the whales live in has fundamentally changed – we know now of a myriad of other threats facing whales, and whaling in the context of all of those is not acceptable.

The IWC needs to end the sham of 'scientific whaling', and can start by properly enforcing whale sanctuaries, such as the Southern Ocean.

The new threats to cetaceans need to be assessed and addressed, and ocean protection needs to be made on a precautionary (if in doubt, don't) and ecosystem-based approach. That means big-scale solutions to attempt to build in some resilience to the ocean and its species, and that means setting large areas off limits to all exploitation as 'Marine Reserves'. The uncertain repercussions of climate change do not make such areas less relevant, it just means they need to be on a bigger scale to have a real effect. Globally, scientific opinion suggests that somewhere between 20 and 50% of our oceans needs to be protected in this way. At the moment ocean protection is languishing at less than one per cent of the world's seas – there is a long way to go. Perhaps a good first step would be giving the Southern Ocean the full protection it deserves.

Finally the IWC needs to actively engage with and promote the true long-term sustainable use of whales that is the whale watching industry.

2) National governments

Individual governments need to enforce protection for cetaceans – starting with the legislation that already exists!

They need to work to minimize the other threats to cetaceans, such as fishing, pollution, shipping, development and noise, and be stronger in holding other nations to account in meeting international agreements.

Governments must also meet their own targets on reducing emissions to minimize the effects of climate change. And to preserve areas of ocean from the inevitable effects of climate change, countries really need to continue creating protected areas, crucially large, fully-protected international Marine Reserves.

Finally, it is crucial to close loopholes that allow the routine killing of cetaceans by 'legal means', such as indiscriminate methods of fishing.

3) Individuals

We must keep our politicians on their toes, and call them to account. Do your elected representatives know what you think about whaling? Do you know what they think about whaling?

Politicians can be asked to back all the things our governments need to do to give effective protection, in national and international waters: to back the creation of protected reserves; to call the government to action on failures and continued whaling, and get your government to take the lead in strong international laws and position.

Simple, day-to-day considerations like reducing your own impact (all that rubbish in the oceans, pollutants in the water, and CO_2 emissions come from somewhere, you know!).

Also, buy responsibly-caught fish: make sure what you eat is caught in a selective and sustainable way. As a rule, try and go for line-caught and local fisheries, and avoid things that are endangered, caught in very big nets, bottom trawls or come from the other side of the planet.

Support whale watching on holidays (remember, you don't even have to get on a boat if you don't want to).

Whilst the option of a boycott of any nation whaling seems a sensible one, I would urge a note of caution. By all means make the decision yourself if you want to buy a TV from Japan, or some fish from Iceland, but remember that not everyone in those

countries is advocating or supporting whaling; in fact it is those that speak out and question whaling in these countries who will largely be responsible for ending it there. Remember too that in other countries we have our own blatant failings in protecting species. My main piece of advice on any personal boycott, is to make sure that those concerned (company, embassy, etc.) know what you're doing and why – so back it up with some communication too!

The future cetacean situation?

Given how much we don't know about cetacean populations, and how they are made up and interact, it's very difficult to make any meaningful judgements based on total population numbers. It may be that a number that sounds very healthy and robust belies a myriad of problems which are exacerbated by separated populations by location, feeding preferences, size, or social activity. Populations that are reduced also run the very real risk of dipping below a crucial threshold point at which they are no longer viable. This is what seems to have happened with passenger pigeons, and probably also to northwest Atlantic cod stocks.

As numbers become ever smaller, genetic diversity is also constrained, which causes direct problems in terms of reproductive ability, and also longer term problems over having sufficiently deep gene pools to adapt to future change – in decades and centuries to come. Looking even further forward, by diminishing the genetic stocks of cetaceans (and, of course this applies equally to gorillas, giraffes, and Galápagos tortoises) we are also compromising their ability to evolve in the future to meet changing environmental demands. If we want our future world to have healthy populations of whales, dolphins and porpoises, then we really need to start changing our ways now.

Image on facing page:
Minke whale surfaces in the English Channel

Scalloway minke

In June 2007, in the same harbour in Scalloway, in Shetland where I'd seen my first ever cetaceans as a child, a rather distressed looking young minke whale was clearly very disoriented. It didn't just look ill, it looked in severe trouble, visibly emaciated and with something that looked like a rope constricting its throat and cutting into its flesh. Sadly the whale died a day or so later, its pathetic lifeless body washed up on shore amongst the flotsam and jetsam. It had been killed by rubbish, a plastic strap (an innocuous piece of trash like you get on large cardboard boxes) which presumably the whale had swum into when it was younger, and smaller, was what had cut into its flesh and restricted its throat. It can't have been a pleasant death, growing slowly into the choking noose that would kill you.

To me that minke whale, a species that is still hunted commercially, 'scientifically' and in nets, illustrates exactly that in a world where we are causing so many other perils to our whales, dolphins, and porpoises, directly killing them is no longer necessary or acceptable. Fishing nets, pollution, noise, shipping traffic, coastal developments, underwater cables, over-fishing, and climate change are all making life increasingly difficult for our cetaceans. On top of all of the threats we humans are creating for the world's remaining whale populations, directly killing them is adding fatal injury to insult. It's the one threat to whales we can, and should, end immediately.

So, saving the whales doesn't just mean stopping pointing harpoons at them, but it is the right place to start.

Fin

Acknowledgements

Big thanks to Kat at Beautiful Books for all the support and making my first foray into writing comparatively stress-free.

Thanks too to my colleagues at Greenpeace UK, particularly David and Anita for enthusiasm and encouragement, Cat for keeping me relatively sane, Niall for painful puns, and Daphne for her perky pictorial professionalism.

Lastly, and most importantly, thanks to Dave for his endless patience reading through all the drafts, and for generally putting up with me, too.

References

1   Darwin, C. R. *On the origin of species by means of natural selection, or the preservation of favoured races in the struggle for life.* John Murray, 1859

2   Scoresby, W. *Memorials of the Sea,* 1835

3   *Scientists capture giant squid on camera; first images of creature live in the wild.* MSNBC News. September 28 2005. http://www.msnbc.msn.com/id/9503272/

4   Fishery Board for Scotland Scientific Investigations, III. 1928, p. 4–5

5   Johnsen, A. O. and J. N. Tønnessen. *The History of Modern Whaling,* trans. R. I. Christopherson. Berkeley, 1982 p. 268

6   Roberts, Callum. *The Unnatural History of the Sea.* Island Press, 2007

7   Salvesen, T. E. *Journal of the Royal Society of Arts,* 1912, p. 523

8/9 International Convention for the Regulation of Whaling. Washington, December 2, 1946

10   Francis, Daniel. *A History of World Whaling.* Viking, 1990

11   Breiwick, J. M. et al. 'Simulated population trajectories for northwest Atlantic humpback whales 1865–1980'. Fifth biennial Conference on Biology of Marine Mammals. Boston Abstract. 1983, p. 14

12   Branch, T. A. et al. 'Evidence for increases in Antarctic blue whales based on Bayesian modelling'. *Marine Mammal Science 20* (2004): 726–754

13   Brown, M. and J. May. *The Greenpeace Story.* Dorling Kindersley Ltd., 1989, p. 39

14/15 Mulvaney, Kieran. *The Whaling Season: An Inside Account of the Struggle to Stop Commercial Whaling.* Shearwater Books, 2003, p. 58

16   *The Japanese Ministry of Agriculture,* Forestry and Fisheries, April 2008

17   St. Kitts and Nevis Declaration, IWC/58, 2006

18   Chair's report of the 57th annual meeting of the International Whaling Commission, 2005. p. 7

19   Jeremy Vine Show, *BBC Radio 2,* 18 January 2008

20   *Humane Society demonstrates ignorance.* Institute of Cetacean Research, press release. 25 July, 2007 http://www.icrwhale.org eng/070725Release.pdf.

21   *Japan admits trading whale votes.* BBC News. July 18 2001. http://www.icrwhale.org/eng/070725Release.pdf

22   *Opinion Poll on research whaling*, Commissioned by Greenpeace Japan, and prepared by Nippon Research Center Ltd., 2008 on http://www.greenpeace.org/raw/content/international/press/reports/japanese-opinion-whaling-2008.pdf

23   *Vast Increase of Tourists Booking Whale Watching*, Iceland review, 9 April 2008. http://www.icelandreview.com/icelandreview/search/news/Default.asp?ew_0_a_id=303994

24   Adams, Douglas. *Last Chance to See.* Pan Macmillan Ltd., 1991

25   Ransom, A. M. and Boris Worm. *'Rapid worldwide depletion of predatory fish communities'.* Nature 423 (2003): 280–283

26   Pauly, Daniel and Kristin Kaschner. *Competition Between Marine Mammals and Fisheries: Food for Thought.* University of British Columbia, 2004

27   UN FAO, *Review of the state of world marine fishery resources,* FAO technical paper 457. 2005

28   Roberts, Callum. *The Unnatural History of the Sea.* Island Press, 2007, p. 340

29   Worm, Boris et al. *'Impacts of biodiversity loss on ocean ecosystem services'.* Science 314 (2006): 787–790

30   Read, A. J. et al. *Bycatches of marine mammals in US fisheries, and a first attempt to estimate the magnitude of global marine mammal bycatch.* SC/55/BC5. Report of the IWC. 2003

31   Clover, Charles. *The End of the Line.* Ebury Press, 2004

32   Atkinson, A. et al. 'Long-term decline in krill stock and increase in salps within the Southern Ocean'. Nature 423: 100–103

Image References

With special respect to the talented and resourceful Greenpeace photographers for capturing such stunningly eloquent images.

Greenpeace **3**
Kate Davison/Greenpeace **6–7**
Scott Portelli/Greenpeace **8**
Doug Perrine/Seapics.com **12**
Doc White/Seapics.com **19**
Scott Portelli/Greenpeace **22**
D. Vienne/Greenpeace **28**
Greenpeace **32**
Daniel Betrá/Greenpeace **34**
Armin Maywald/Greenpeace **38**
Willie Mackenzie **44**
Lizzie Barber/Greenpeace **48–49**
Hiroya Minakuchi/Seapics.com **51**
Daniel Betrá/Greenpeace **56**
Greenpeace **60–61**
Kate Davison/Greenpeace **66**
Greenpeace **71**
Kate Davison/Greenpeace **74**
Kate Davison/Greenpeace **80**
Daniel Betrá/Greenpeace **82**
John Cunningham/Greenpeace **88**
Jean Paul Ferrero/Greenpeace **94**
John Cunningham/Greenpeace **96–97**
Nick Cobbing/Greenpeace **101**
Nick Cobbing/Greenpeace **104**
Kate Davison/Greenpeace **110**
Fred Scott/Greenpeace **112**
Kate Davison/Greenpeace **118**
John Cunningham/Greenpeace **124–5**
Noda Masaya/Greenpeace **126**

Natalie Behring/Greenpeace **130**
Daniel Betrá/Greenpeace **134**
John Hyde/Greenpeace **136–7**
Michael S. Nolan/Seapics.com **142**
Willie Mackenzie **148**
Lizzie Barber/Greenpeace **154**
Bob Cranston/Seapics.com **158**
Igor Gavrilov/Greenpeace **160–1**
Kate Davison/Greenpeace **167**
Alan Greig/Greenpeace **171**
Greenpeace **173**
Roger Grace/Greenpeace **176**
Nick Cobbing/Greenpeace **178**
Kate Davison/Greenpeace **184**
Lizzie Barber/Greenpeace **186**
Daniel Betrá/Greenpeace **192**

More, more, more

If you want to know more about some of
the issues mentioned in the text, then
here is a totally arbitrary list of suggested
further sources of information.

Books

Dolin, Eric Jay. *Leviathan, the History of
Whaling in America,* W. W. Norton & Co.
Inc., 2007

Hoyt, Eric. *Marine Protected Areas, for
Whales, Dolphins and Porpoises,*
Earthscan, 2005

Lazarus, Sarah. *Troubled Waters: The
Changing Fortunes of Whales and
Dolphins,* Natural History Museum,
London, 2006

Mulvaney, Kieran. *The Whaling Season:
An Inside Account of the Struggle to Stop
Commercial Whaling,* Shearwater Books,
2003

Roberts, Professor Callum. *The Unnatural
History of the Sea,* Island Press, 2007

Simmonds, Mark. *Whales and Dolphins
of the World,* New Holland Publishers Ltd.,
2004

Wyler, Rex. *Greenpeace: an insider's
account,* Rodale International, 2004

Reports

General threats
Whales in a degraded ocean
Greenpeace, 2001

Noise
Oceans of Noise, Whale and Dolphin
Conservation Society (WDCS), 2004

**Failures of Conservation for
UK cetaceans**
*The Conservation of British Cetaceans:
a review of the threats and protection
afforded to whales, dolphins and
porpoises in UK waters,* WDCS, 2007

Climate Change
*Whales in Hot Water: the impact of a
changing climate on whales, dolphins and
porpoises,* WWF and WDCS, 2007

Pollution
*Global chemical pollution and the hunting
of whales, dolphins and porpoises,*
Environmental Investigation Agency (EIA),
2004 http://www.eia-international.org/
files/reports84-1.pdf

By-catch
Review of cetacean bycatch in pelagic
trawls and other fisheries in the Northeast
Atlantic, WDCS, 2004 http://www.wdcs.
org/submissions_bin/neteffect.pdf

Eating whales
*We Don't Buy It! Nippon Suisan, Maruha
and Kyokuyo's continuing support for
Japan's whaling,* EIA, 2008

Welfare
*Troubled Waters – a review of the welfare
implications of modern whaling activities,*
published by the World Society for the
Protection of Animals (WSPA), 2004.

Small cetacean hunts
EIA reports
The Forgotten Whales. Hunting Baird's
beaked whales in Japan's coastal waters
http://www.eia-international.org/files/
reports56-1.pdf

Stop the Dall's disaster
http://www.eia-international.org/files/
reports119-1.pdf

Vote buying
Japan's "Vote Consolidation Operation"
at the International Whaling Commission,
Third Millennium Foundation, Inc., 2007

Websites

Whaling statistics
Whale catch history from 1910 onwards
http://luna.pos.to/whale/sta.html

Greenpeace
www.greenpeace.org.uk

Environmental Investigation Agency
www.eia-international.org

International Fund for Animal Welfare
www.ifaw.org

**World Society for the Protection of
Animals**
www.wspa.org.uk

Whale and Dolphin Conservation Society
www.wdcs.org

The end ?